Are you a DINK (Double Income, No Kids) who likes to SCUBA (Self-Contained Underwater Breathing Apparatus)? Do you drive a FIAT *(Fabbrica Italiana Automobili Torino)* or use a computer MODEM (MOdulator-DEModulator)? Are your all-time favorite shows *The Man from U.N.C.L.E.* and *M*A*S*H?*

Well, whether or not you SWAK your letters, address them with ZIP codes, and mail them ASAP to avoid a SNAFU, it just proves that you can't avoid acronyms. This handy linguistic shorthand is an inescapable part of our daily lives.

Indeed, it's the age of the acronym, and *Acronymania* celebrates the phenomenon by presenting a plethora of truncated organizations (NOW), brand names (LEGO), military expressions (AWOL), medical terminology (GOMER), and even foreign intrigue (SMERSH).

Crack open this entertaining and informative volume and you'll discover some of the cleverest acronyms ever coined, such as the British crime-tracking computer aptly called HOLMES (Home Office Large Major Enquiry System), the U.S. Navy's LOBSTER (Long-term Ocean Bottom Settlement Test for Engineering Research), and many more. As you browse through the pages of *Acronymania*, remember: WYSIWYG (What You See Is What You Get)!

"Delightful! Original! New! Here's a unique parade through many acronymic nuances. Acronymically, that spells Don Hauptman. Who else but he could so brightly illuminate the mysteries of the acronym?"

—Richard Lederer, author of *More Anguished English*

LAUREL

HOW WELL DO YOU KNOW YOUR ABC'S?

What do the following acronyms stand for?

1. **GIGO**
2. **laser**
3. **radar**
4. **POSSLQ**
5. Navy **SEAL** units
6. **NECCO** wafers

ACRONYMANIA

ANSWERS:

1. **G**arbage **I**n—**G**arbage **O**ut 2. **L**ight **A**mplification by **S**timulated **E**mission of **R**adiation 3. **RA**dio **D**etection **A**nd **R**anging 4. **P**erson(s) of **O**pposite **S**ex **S**haring **L**iving **Q**uarters 5. **SE**a-**A**ir-**L**and 6. **N**ew **E**ngland **C**onfectionery **CO**mpany

ACRONYMANIA

A Celebratory Roundup Of Nomenclature Yielding Mischief: Abbreviations, Neologisms, Initialisms, Acronyms!

Don Hauptman

LAUREL

A LAUREL BOOK

Published by
Dell Publishing
a division of
Bantam Doubleday Dell Publishing Group, Inc.
1540 Broadway
New York, New York 10036

ISBN: 0-440-21160-3

Printed in the United States of America

Published simultaneously in Canada

July 1993

10 9 8 7 6 5 4 3 2 1

OPM

Acknowledgments

Special thanks and appreciation to the acronym enthusiasts and scholars who generously shared with me their collections and insights:

Professor John Algeo, Professor Leonard Ashley, Chris Cole, Paul Dickson, Dr. Sterling Eisiminger, John Kremer, Ed Lucaire, Tom McArthur, Professor Don Nilsen, Professor Félix Rodríguez González, Professor Ralph Slovenko, Brad Templeton (and the many witty contributors to his humor bulletin board on the GEnie network), and the staff of Gale Research, Detroit.

Thanks also to:

Dr. Frank Abate, Gary Alexander, Ira N. Bachrach, Steven L. Baggish, Dr. James H. Boren, Francesca Bucca, Jo-Ann M. Burns, Fred Cookinham, A. Ross Eckler, Susan Ferraro, Michelle Fram-Cohen, Dr. Robert Goodman, David Grambs, Gary Greenberg, Deb Greenblatt, Dr. Anne M. Greenfeld, Dr. Robert Hauptman, George M. Hollenback, Professor Nicholas Howe, Claire D. Hughes, Dave Kahn, Michelle Kamhi, Ted Kikoler, Dr. Richard Lederer, Joyce Lempel, Matt Manning, Curt Monash, Bob Nelson, Craig Packard, Kay Powell, Mary Beth Protomastro, Professor Victor Raskin, Professor Allen Walker Read, John W. Reiser, Professor Robert Rennick, Dr. Hans Rollmann, Laura Sachs, Sandy Sandfort, Rob Schleifer, Tom Sheehan, Dr. Włodzimierz Sobkowiak, Chris Tame, Ben Teague, Lydia Wilen, Cathy Young.

I wish I could claim credit for coining *ACRONYMANIA* (pronounced "ak-ro-nih-MAY-nee-uh"), which I have shamelessly appropriated for the title of this book. This ingenious blend-word has been coined independently by many creative people. Two friends named in the above list suggested it as the title. My research turned up numerous mentions in articles dating back twenty-five years or more. My appreciation to all these clever punsters, known and unknown.

Finally, my thanks to the colleagues and friends who exercised patience during the many months that I was **w**orking **o**n **m**y **b**ook—or **WOMB,** for short! It was an embryonic process.

Contents

Contents

Initial Remarks

❖

A Number Of Minor Introductory Ephemera (ANOMIE)

"Copy this **ASAP**!" "They're both **WASP**s." "In this town, everyone has a **NIMBY** attitude." "What a **snafu**!"

Acronyms are all around. **L**ike **i**t **o**r **n**ot (or **LION**, for short), these handy abbreviations, pronounceable as words and crafted from the initial components of other words, are an integral part of the marvelous English language we use every day.

Indeed, so subtly do they creep into our communications that we often employ acronyms without even being aware that we are doing so. From **scuba** to **yuppie**, from **ZIP** Codes to ***M*A*S*H***, acronyms are a part of our lives.

One day, I phoned a theater that had announced a play with a limited engagement.

"I'd like to order two tickets for Friday evening."

"**S**old **o**ut **f**or **t**he **e**ntire **r**un," barked the reservation taker.

"Do you realize," I riposted, "that what you just said spells **SOFTER**?"

She hung up. But the incident proves that acronyms can appear in the most unexpected places.

Yet despite the ubiquity of this remarkable linguistic and cultural phenomenon, no book devoted to the subject (with the exception of dictionaries of abbreviations intended for reference) has ever been written.

Until now.

ACRONYMANIA has arrived to fill this urgent need. At long last, here is the official, quasi-definitive work on this pervasive yet sadly neglected topic. For good measure, the volume you hold also contains selected examples of other types of abbreviations and linguistic condensations of all sorts. All festooned with explanations, anecdotes, and fascinating trivia that will provide stimulating party conversation for years to come.

Knowledge of linguistic shorthand is essential to understand world events and achieve literacy, both basic and "cultural." The media often cite abbreviations, including acronyms. Sometimes, however, a reporter doesn't bother to explain what the short form represents. As a consequence, mysterious combinations of letters can puzzle the reader or listener.

For example, to keep abreast of world events during the past few years, Americans have had to be familiar with **NASA**, **OPEC**, **SALT**, **OSHA**, **NAFTA**, and scores of other acronyms.

But how many people know that **SWAPO** is the **S**outh**w**est **A**frican **P**eople's **O**rganization, a Marxist guerrilla group opposed to Pretoria's control of Namibia? Or that the scary-sounding **Slorc** is the **S**tate **L**aw and **O**rder **R**estoration **C**ouncil of Myanmar (formerly Burma), which has been accused of assorted brutalities and human rights violations?

Like many of the best things in life—including sex, food, and personal computers—acronyms are not exclusively practical and serious. They also have their fun side.

For lovers of language and wordplay—logophiles and verbivores and devotees of recreational linguistics—acronyms can be a fascinating pastime.

Many specimens are clever, witty, and amusing. They can be neatly and suprisingly appropriate. Or they can be unintentionally—and sometimes hilariously—*in*appropriate. Original, freshly minted acronyms can score a satiric point or serve as mocking expressions of protest and anger toward government agencies and other faceless institutions.

In the pages that follow, we'll explore this fascinating universe and examine both its serious and its humorous facets. Here is a preview.

A Guide to the Journey Ahead

Why acronyms? As civilization and technology advance, entities and concepts proliferate, from space shuttles to demographic subgroups. To designate all sorts of stuff that did not previously exist, we must devise *new* words, or grant new meanings to old ones.

Acronyms are one of several methods available to name all these new things.

Contrary to many linguistic gurus, pundits, and curmudgeons who decry the presumed perils of excessive abbreviation, I am convinced that the phenomenon is largely *positive*. The functions of abbreviations and acronyms, and the benefits they bestow upon humankind, along with a forum for opposing views, will be found in Chapter 1.

An acronym is a *pronounceable abbreviation*. As long as it is read and spoken as a single unit rather than letter by letter, it's an acronym, whether it spells a meaningful "real" word *or* a meaningless "nonword." Chapters 1 and 2 contain terms and definitions and a classification system. Chapter 2 also outlines our "rules" for proper acronym formation and supplies a rating method to enable us to evaluate acronyms and to differentiate a good coinage from a bad one.

With our **A**cronymic **T**ime **O**rienting **M**achine (**ATOM**), we'll travel into the past and examine the long and glorious history of abbreviation, and its intriguing lore. Synchronize your watches at the start of Chapter 3.

As we've observed, acronyms often enter the language and everyday discourse stealthily. Thus, you may not even be aware of the acronymic origins of some of the words you use. In Chapter 4, you'll find fascinating stories of acronyms that evolved into legitimate lower-case English words. And the truth about all those words that people *think* are acronyms but really aren't!

Next, in Chapter 5, we present some of the most appealing acronymic names of organizations, projects, and causes.

Chapter 6 offers enticing specimens from the vocabularies of numerous professions—from medicine to business and finance, and from the military services to entertainment and literature. You'll find acronymic names of people and places. What happens when an abbreviated name of a business or institution or nation *changes*. And some peculiar choices that resulted in unintended—and often outrageous—consequences.

Of course, acronyms occur in other languages. We cite examples from Russian, German, French, and other tongues, with translations, in Chapter 7.

Chapter 8 examines the humorous side of the phenomenon. Barbed and devilish redefinitions. Clever acronyms that aren't part of our language, but *should* be. And—hang on!—a fast-paced excursion into multiple acronymia.

Chapter 9 unveils a host of entertaining diversions for kids and grown-ups, including an acronym party game, acrostic verse, how to communicate exclusively in initials, and other treats.

Our linguistic safari concludes in Chapter 10 with "the acronym acronym," the longest examples, and the presentation of our awards for the best and most imaginative acronymic creations of all time (well, maybe).

If by that point your acronymic hunger is not sated, Appendix II supplies a bibliography of additional references and source materials.

Caveats, Disclaimers, and Such

I have spent many arduous but rewarding hours plowing through hundreds of sources and thousands of abbreviations, culling only the finest, museum-quality specimens for your edification and amusement.

My criteria were simple. I searched for acronyms and other abbreviations that struck me as appropriate to their intended purposes, and those that seemed wildly, egregiously, or hilariously *in*appropriate. I sought, and devised, acronyms that might provoke a smile or a laugh. And I plucked samples that would illustrate a point, convey some knowledge, or provoke the exclamation "Wow, I didn't know *that*!"

Note that a specific acronym may (and most likely does) have *more than one* possible meaning or full form—even if only one is cited in this volume. These qualifications help explain why you might not see your favorite abbreviation here, nor find an explanation for that set of cryptic letters about which you've been scratching your head.

Hence this caution: *ACRONYMANIA* is intended

as a popular, entertaining book. Though carefully researched and (I hope) accurate, it is *not* a dictionary or encyclopedia, and in no way claims to be a complete listing of acronyms or abbreviations.

As noted above, I have included in Appendix II a listing of some of the key sources and references I consulted. If you need to determine what a specific abbreviation stands for, or if for any other reason you require a comprehensive reference work, please consult one of these dictionaries at your library.

Beyond **a**ll **r**easonable **d**oubt (**BARD**), this book contains **l**ots **o**f **i**nteresting **s**tuff (**LOIS**). In its pages, you'll discover **a** **l**ittle **o**f **e**verything (**ALOE**). **F**or **a** **v**ariety **o**f **r**easons (**FAVOR**), it will give you **a**n **e**normous **s**ense **o**f **p**leasure (**AESOP**). Of course, **t**hat's **a**ll **t**hat **u**ltimately **m**atters (**TATUM**)!

After you have closed the covers of *ACRONYMANIA*, I trust that approval will be your initial reaction.

Don Hauptman
New York, N.Y.

CHAPTER 1

❖

Why Acronyms Recur, Benefiting Literacy Everywhere (WARBLE)

Are acronyms and abbreviations a force for good or evil? In this chapter, we shall consider arguments both pro and con.

But first, we must understand the various methods of linguistic compression. We thus need a classification scheme, or *taxonomy.*

According to a group of Indiana linguists, a taxonomy should be "**p**olytheoretical, **u**niversal, **r**ich, **d**efinitive, **u**niform, and **e**xpandable." Coincidentally enough, this formula spells **PURDUE**, the name of their university.

By the way, if you really want to be trendy, call it *systematics* instead of taxonomy. Good grief! It's tough to keep up even with the terminology for terminology!

Note that fitting every specimen into a neat pigeonhole is impossible; boundaries blur, and some examples qualify for more than one category.

In addition to the devices discussed in the following sections, other abbreviation techniques are covered in our history lesson, Chapter 3.

A Taxonomy of Linguistic Condensation

Clippings

The clipping is the most obvious way of shortening language. It may have begun ages ago in everyday conversation, as speakers truncated words and expressions to save time and effort. Linguists have unkindly labeled them *stump words.* Some clippings are still considered informal or colloquial, while others have been "legitimized" as formal English.

Consider a few familiar examples: *bra, condo, copter, deli, mayo, memo, photo, prefab.*

Often, the shortened form becomes more common than the longer form. This happened to *gym* for *gymnasium, stereo* for *stereophonic, ad* (the British prefer *advert*) for *advertisement,* and *vet* for *veteran* (or for *veterinarian*).

Sometimes the clipped version of the word becomes so accepted that the original form is abandoned or even forgotten. How many people today know, for example, that *piano* comes from *pianoforte,* that a *wig* was a *periwig,* or that a *quack* (phony physician) was once a *quacksalver*? Similarly, *bus* is from *omnibus, zoo* from *zoological garden,* and *pants* from *pantaloons.*

In "black English" and street slang, this process

creates new words. For example, *dis* (or *diss*), a verb meaning "to disrespect," is a clipping of *disapprove* or *dismiss*. And *def*, a term of high praise, may derive from *definite* or *definitive*. A more surprising etymology, proposed by some lexicographers, is that the word is borrowed from West Indian English for *death*.

To describe this type of shortening, linguists and other scholars employ a specialized and impressive terminology.

Decapitating or lopping off the *front* of the word is called fore-clipping or *aphesis* (pronounced "AF-ih-sis") or *apheresis* ("uh-FAIR-uh-sis"). The two terms have slightly different meanings, but not enough to worry about. Examples: *phone* (from *telephone*), *plane* (*airplane*), *possum* (*opossum*), *round* (*around*). Although these short forms all coexist with their longer parents, the shorter form can supplant the longer one, as with *cello* (which once was *violincello*) and *special* (formerly *especial*). Sometimes an apostrophe takes the place of the missing syllable (e.g., *'round*), but usually it too soon disappears.

Dropping the *middle* syllable or sound is *syncope* (pronounced "SIN-koh-pee"). An example is *fortnight* (which once was *fourteen-night*).

Deleting the *final* part of the word is back-clipping or *apocope* (pronounced "uh-POCK-uh-pee"). This variety is the most common. Examples: *auto, dorm, exam, fax, lab.* And *curio* (from *curiosity*), *celeb* (for *celebrity*), *fan* (interestingly enough, from *fanatic*), *perk* (from *perquisite*), *porn* or *porno* (from *pornography*).

Sometimes, albeit rarely, both the front *and* the back of the word vanish. Familiar examples include *flu* for *influenza* and *fridge* for *refrigerator.* Perhaps because it occurs so infrequently, no intimidating term seems to exist for this phenomenon.

In a related form of condensation called an *ellipsis,* or *clipped compound,* entire words vanish. Most often, in a noun/adjective combination, the noun is lost. Thus, *cable television* becomes *cable,* a *compact car* a *compact,* a *pickup truck* a *pickup.* This process can occur simultaneously with the clipping of syllables. A *temporary worker* becomes a *temp,* a *substitute* evolves into a *sub,* a *physical examination* turns into a *physical exam* and then a *physical.*

Here is a striking example of this evolutionary development. In the 1820s, *cabriolet,* a horse-drawn carriage, was commonly back-clipped to *cab.* The first mechanical fare meters were installed in these vehicles, which were then dubbed *taximeter cabs.* Soon, of course, the horseless carriage replaced the horse and buggy. The word was clipped to *taxicab,* and then split in two. Today, both halves, *taxi* and *cab,* coexist and are used interchangeably.

As with clothing, trendy abbreviations can go out of style. Here's a small sampling of formerly fashionable clippings that are now obsolete: *phiz* (face, from *physiognomy*), *ush* (for *usher,* as a verb), and *insurge* (as a verb).

Blends

A blend is a merging or fusion of two words, which usually—though not always—shortens matters.

Familiar illustrations include **brunch**, **smog**, and **telecast**. More recently, the lexicon of blend words has expanded to include **camcorder**, **glasphalt**, **dancercize**, **bit** (from **b**inary dig**it**), and **Chunnel** (the English **Ch**annel t**unnel**).

Products in search of catchy names often seize upon a blend. **Spam** (**sp**iced h**am**), **Swatch** (**Sw**iss w**atch**), **Velcro** (fasteners invented in Switzerland; the name is from the French ***vel**ours,* velvet, and ***cro**ché,* hooked).

The gossip columns of Walter Winchell and the pages of *Time* magazine popularized blends both jocular and serious: **cinemactress**, **guesstimate**, **frauditor**, **genethics**, **infanticipating** (for pregnant).

A blend can be constructed from *any* of the components of the original words: the front of the first word and the back of the second, or the whole of either, as in the preceding examples, or the *initial* syllables of *both* words, as in **sitcom** (**sit**uation **com**edy), **minicam** (**mini**ature **cam**era), and **pixel** (from **pic**ture **el**ement). Caution: **Hydrox** is not just a brand of cookie, but also **hydr**ogen-**ox**ygen fuel.

Lewis Carroll, in his *Alice* books, coined many

such inventive blends, including **mimsy** and **slithy**. Several of his coinages have entered the language, most notably **chortle** (from **ch**uckle and sn**ort**). Carroll called his neologistic blends *portmanteau words* (from a portmanteau, a traveling bag that opens into two compartments; hence "two meanings packed up into one word"). An equally evocative term, once more common, is *telescope word.*

Contractions and elisions

A contraction is an abbreviation that omits one or more letters from within a word, thus collapsing or imploding it. The process is similar to syncope, discussed above.

As we will see in Chapter 3, contractions originated long ago. Although some early conventions fell into disuse, many of the forms of abbreviation we use today evolved from ancient languages.

Examples of contractions that retain the first and last letters include the familiar honorifics **Dr.** and **Mr.** (which are always pronounced in their full forms). **Mrs.** is short for *mistress.* As for **Ms.**, it has gradually won acceptance, despite the carping of traditionalists that it is harsh-sounding, artificial, and illegitimate (unlike its counterparts, it has no full form). Some holdouts still refuse to use it.

Contractions that omit vowels and some consonants include **atty.**, **bldg.**, **mfg.**, and **hdqrs**.

Many contractions in everyday use, such as *can't* and *I'm,* drop a vowel—a phenomenon called *elision.* Some elided words are slang, including *'bout* and *'nuff* (for *enough*). *Ne'er* is a now-archaic (and still poetic) form for *never.* Also obsolete are *th'are* for *they are, p'raps* for *perhaps,* and *ta'en* for *taken.*

In written form, the apostrophe and the period served as devices that substituted for the omitted characters, thus indicating that the word was an abbreviation. This process was not universal, however, and even today the British style is *Dr* and *Mr* —omitting the period.

Initialisms

In the simplest type of initialism, a single letter represents a word. Examples: **K** for *Kilobyte,* **N** for *North,* and **p.** for *page.*

Obviously, however, this approach has its limits. With only twenty-six letters, duplication and confusion can quickly result. So most initialisms are composed of *several* letters. Examples abound, so familiar that they need no explanation: **C.D.**, **I.Q.**, **O.J.**, **C.P.R.**, **E.S.P.**, **I.U.D.**, **L.S.D.**, **B.Y.O.B.**, **T.G.I.F.**

In contrast to the acronym, which we shall examine momentarily, the initialism is read or sounded out *letter by letter,* a process sometimes called *literation.*

Some of our initialisms are borrowed from Latin —e.g., **e.g.** (for example, for example!). The letters stand for *exempli gratia,* "for the sake of example." Some writers, unaware of the meaning of e.g., misuse the term, confusing it with **i.e.**, *id est,* "that is."

Other everyday terms derived from Latin are **A.M.**

and P.M. (from ***a**nte* and ***p**ost **m**eridiem*, not "meridian"); **M.O.** (***m**odus **o**perandi*); and **Q.E.D.** (***q**uod **e**rat **d**emonstrandum*), which is triumphantly announced at the conclusion of a proof and which might be translated as "so there!"

In abbreviation, as in all things, conventions differ. Case in point: although both the United States and Great Britain practice ***d**o **i**t **y**ourself,* the initialism **D.I.Y.** is in general use only over there.

Some abbreviations derive not from the first letters of a series of words but from selected letters of a *single* word. Such a "one-word initialism" is **PJs**, from the initials of each syllable of **p**a**j**amas. Others include **T.V.** and **O.D.** (**o**ver**d**ose). The first two letters of ***id**entification* yield **I.D.** The now almost archaic expression for secrecy, *on the **Q.T.***, derives from the first and last letters of ***q**uie**t***.

Another subspecies is the type of initialism that, because the sound of each letter is homophonous with (sounds the same as) a syllable, is pronounceable as a word. This variety might be labeled an "initialism word." For example, **M.C./emcee**. If the preceding explanation seems a bit opaque, fear not. We will study this animal more closely later on.

Acronyms

An acronym—our favorite form—is a type of abbreviation in which the first letters or first syllables of a series of words are linked to create a *new* word.

Acronyms are distinguished from initialisms by the fact that they are always pronounceable as words. For example, **R.P.M.** is an initialism, while **NATO** is an acronym. You will find no shortage of additional specimens in the pages that follow.

Although acronyms have been around for millennia (see Chapter 3), the word itself is of surprisingly recent vintage. According to one account, a Bell Laboratories researcher working on war projects in the early 1940s coined the word. Unfortunately, AT&T's archivists cannot confirm the story.

"Acronym" made its public debut in the February 1943 issue of the journal *American Notes & Queries.* A reader named Basil Davenport responded to a letter published the previous month that had asked about "the concoction of new words from the first letters." To quote Mr. Davenport's historic reply, the coinage "is useful, and clear to anyone who knows a little Greek."

Specifically, the little classical Greek one needs to know is *akros,* "tip" or "top," and *onyma,* "name." Among several suggested literal translations: "tip name," "high word," and "peak name." All of these English renderings sound awkward and clumsy, which only serves to confirm the need for a brand-new term, and the wisdom of coining it from classical elements.

Based on its etymology alone, "acronym" *could* be construed to mean an abbreviation that is pronounced either as a word *or* by its component letters. But usage has clearly shifted to favor the first definition exclusively. "Initialism," as we have noted, is the proper term for the latter. Terminological confusion, however, is rife—as we shall shortly see.

But if acronyms are thousands of years old, what were they called *before* 1943?

Prior to the invention of the new term, acronyms were often not differentiated from other forms of abbreviation. When they were, they were sometimes referred to as *acrostics,* and were so defined in dictionaries. This archaic usage continued even after the new word was coined. Some language books published in the 1950s, and even as late as the 1970s, use "acrostic" rather than acronym. (Today, an acrostic is a verse form in which the initial letters of each line create a phrase; see Chapters 3 and 9.)

Pronounceable abbreviations have also been dubbed "protograms," "abecedisms," "letter words," "polysynthetic words," and a plethora of other terms.

The eloquent **KISS** rule ("**K**eep **i**t **s**imple, **s**tupid," and variants) applies here. All these coinages are unnecessary, and only serve to blur the distinctions among the various types of abbreviation. "Acronym" suits us fine.

In a 1962 *American Speech* article, Professor S. V. Baum of Brooklyn College grouped acronyms, according to their structure, into four categories he called "orders." Although provocative, his meticulous taxonomy, and various attempts by others, need not concern us here. Regrettably, such classifications (even ours) are never perfect. Exceptions that don't fit the schema always pop up with annoying regularity.

Syllabic acronyms

The examples in the preceding section are all *letter acronyms.* Another legitimate type is the *syllabic acronym,* which is crafted from *several consecutive letters* of each word.

Examples include **AMVETS** (**Am**erican **Vet**erans), **NABISCO** (**Na**tional **Bis**cuit **Co**mpany), and **INTELSAT** (**In**ternational **Tel**ecommunications **Sat**ellite Organization).

Some syllabic acronyms have become lower-case words:

moped, from **mo**tor and **ped**al (originally a Swedish coinage)

napalm (**na**phthene and **palm**itate)

motocross (**moto**r and **cross**-country)

hazmat (**haz**ardous **mat**erial, specifically poisons, explosives, and radioactive substances)

telex (**tel**eprinter **ex**change), which has been virtually obsoleted by fax machines and by the . . .

modem (**mo**dulator/**dem**odulator)

Syllabic acronyms are obviously kin to the portmanteau word or blend, which we discussed earlier.

Most such coinages combine the *first* part of one word with the *second* (usually last) part of another (e.g., **motel,** from **mo**tor and ho**tel**), and so are *not* true acronyms. But specimens in which the *first* part of one word combines with the *first* part of another, such as **hi-fi**, **op-ed**, and **COMSAT**, can be categorized either as syllabic acronyms *or* as blends. Take your choice.

Portmanteau words and syllabic acronyms are analogous to the formation of words in Japanese, observes Tom McArthur, editor of the journal *English Today*. "Such acronyms fit easily into Japanese," he notes. The similarities facilitate the worldwide proliferation of coined blends, such as **TEXACO** (**Texa**s **Co**mpany) and **Mavica** (a Japanese brand of **ma**gnetic **vi**deo **ca**mera).

"Every acronym is a blend but not vice versa," observes Chris Cole, a Southern California software entrepreneur and acronym enthusiast. "However, blends usually are constructed from phonemes, while quality acronyms are constructed from initials."

Miscellaneous forms of abbreviation

Many other methods of condensing language have evolved. Not all have been christened with official names, nor do they all fit neatly into our major categories. The meaning and pronunciation of such abbreviations are sometimes less obvious than the standard forms.

Halfway between initialisms and acronyms are

such curious creatures as **STOL** (**s**hort **t**ake**o**ff and **l**anding) and **VTOL** (**v**ertical **t**ake**o**ff and **l**anding). The first letter of each term is pronounced as an initialism, and the remainder as an acronym ("ess-tole" and "vee-tole"). Perhaps the form is echoing the aerodynamics. Or else the manufacturer wanted to avoid "stall"!

Yet another hybrid type of abbreviation combines a letter with a word, as in **A-list**, **H-bomb**, **L-shaped room**, **U-turn**, **U-boat** (from German *Untersee*), **T-square**, **T-bill** (a U.S. **T**reasury bond), **C-note** (a hundred dollars, from the Roman numeral), and **G-man** (from *government*). Or a letter might merge with a number, as with **A-1** (first-rate) and **K-9** (a pun on the homophonous *canine*).

The astronauts who brought back those moon rocks called them **KREEP**. No relation to the infamous Watergate acronym (see page 191), this KREEP is an unusual mixed coinage composed of **K** (the chemical symbol for potassium), **r**are-**e**arth **e**lements, and **p**hosphorus.

As previously noted, English has borrowed abbreviations from other languages, such as **R.S.V.P.** (***r**épondez, **s**'il **v**ous **p**laît*) from French, and, from Latin, **R.I.P.** (***r**equiescat **i**n **p**ace*), **DT**s (***d**elirium **t**remens*), and *pro tem* (short for *pro tempore,* temporarily).

But some of these "loanwords" employ strange devices. For example, **Ph.D.** is from ***Ph**ilosophiae **D**octor,* which explains the seemingly reversed structure of the abbreviation.

Certain symbols can prove unfamiliar and puzzling. A micron (one millionth of a meter) is abbreviated **μ** (the Greek letter *mu,* the equivalent of our M). The letters **lb.** are from the Latin ***libra*** (balance or scales), which also was a unit of weight in ancient Rome. Libra is the origin of the **£** sign, and it's been suggested that the symbol **#** to indicate a pound evolved from a quickly scrawled £. Mathematics and chemistry, among other disciplines, employ a large vocabulary of symbol abbreviations.

The familiar prescription symbol ℞ derives from ***recipe*** (Latin for the verb "to take"), possibly combined with r , the alchemist's symbol for Jupiter, his patron god (some scholars, however, say the extra stroke is just a simple abbreviation mark). And your doctor's scribblings that appear so arcane are apothecary symbols derived from Latin or Greek, such as ʒi for one teaspoon and i/d meaning once a day.

Still another variant form might be called "phonemic abbreviation." In this method, letters are pronounced to simulate words or syllables.

For example, **easy** is informally rendered as **EZ**, and **ex**ce**ss** as **XS**. **BBQ** is short for **b**ar**beq**ue, and **PX** for **p**ost **ex**change. **I.O.U.** puns the latter two of its three letters. **VXL** was once an inscription on lockets. **V** is an older form of **U**; hence the letters were a pun on "**you excel**." Today, users of electronic mail and computer bulletin boards save time and money by communicating "**oh, I see**" with **OIC** and "**be seein' you**" with **BCNU**. These creations have been dubbed *rebuses, letter puns,* and *A.B.C. Language.* For a game based on this principle, turn to Chapter 9, page 246.

Certain abbreviations originated in error. **Tub**erculosis is universally referred to as **T.B.**, but the initialism first stood *not* for the illness but for ***t**ubercle **b**acillus,* the organism that causes it.

Finally, classification can be thorny if we don't know how the short form came about.

"The origins of some abbreviations are obscure," notes Harold K. Hughes in his *Dictionary of Abbreviations in Medicine and the Health Sciences.* For example, phenethicillin potassium is **CVK**, but "only the **K** as the chemical symbol for potassium is suggestive of the meaning." Another now-opaque code Dr. Hughes cites is **DOE**, "whose origin as a name or abbreviation for someone taking illicit drugs is lost in obscurity."

Terminological Confusions and Clarifications

We have noted that the word "acronym" was invented only about 1943 and has since been interpreted in a bewildering variety of ways.

Here, once and for all, are the official facts. Don't believe anyone who tells you different. Listen up:

It's an *initialism* if the letters are sounded individually, and an *acronym* if they create a pronounceable word. The full form—the words constituting the abbreviation—is called the *expansion.* The umbrella term for shortening words to fewer letters (or to symbols) is *abbreviation.*

Unfortunately, misuses are *still* rampant, and proper terminology is often ignored or blurred, causing general confusion.

Often, *any* letter abbreviation is automatically labeled an "acronym." For example, a newspaper reporter called **A.T.M.** (**a**utomatic **t**eller **m**achine) an acronym. Not so! No one pronounces it "atom," so it's unquestionably an initialism. An op-ed essay mulled the question of whether a bunch of international agencies will survive the end of the Cold War. Says the writer: "They make quite a list of acronyms: **NATO, EC, IMF, UN, IBRD, GATT, CSCE, WEU, IAEA**. . . ." Only the first and sixth names on his list are true acronyms.

The difference between an initialism and an acronym can be crucial! Consider the following cautionary tale:

I.R.A. is an initialism when referring to the **I**rish **R**epublican **A**rmy, but an **IRA** (pronounced per Ira Gershwin) is an acronym if one means an **I**ndividual **R**etirement **A**ccount. In 1990, *The Wall Street Journal* reported the scary experience of an American couple, equipped with an Irish surname and living in London. The expatriates' brokerage statements attracted the suspicions of their mail carrier, who spotted envelopes addressed to "Jack O'Brien IRA" and "Barbara O'Brien IRA." After intercepting and opening the envelopes, the police redelivered them, along with an apology, to the startled couple.

Even some scholars and lexicographers, who should know better, are confounded. Titles of some reference volumes (see Appendix II) confuse the terms. One article in an academic journal managed to reverse matters completely, calling an initialism an acronym, and an acronym an initialism!

Blends of all sorts have been erroneously labeled acronyms. Again, a portmanteau word that uses *initial* syllables exclusively (such as **minicam**) may be called a blend, a portmanteau word, *or* a syllabic acronym. But a blend word that merges first and *last* syllables (such as **motel**) is excluded from the category of acronyms.

Yet another source of confusion: some authorities define the term "abbreviation" as a shortened form *other than* an acronym or initialism. One glossary, for example, limits the definition of abbreviation to what it calls "short forms": contractions (such as **qtrs.** for quarters) and clippings (**equip.** for equipment). Still others say an abbreviation is one of the miscellaneous unclassified forms discussed above, such as **Ph.D.** But this distinction seems arbitrary. *The Random House Dictionary* defines abbreviation as "a shortened or contracted form of a word or phrase, used to represent the whole." Abbreviation is thus the inclusive rubric.

Back-formations and "Bacronyms"

Some people call an acronym coined for the purpose of creating a genuine preexisting word a "back-formation." Or, in a cute neologistic blend, a "bacronym." In this paradigm, **UNESCO** would be an acronym, and **CARE** a bacronym.

But does this terminology make sense? Let's find out.

Back-formation is an etymological term for the creation of a new word, most often a verb, by removing an element from an existing *longer* form of that word. Either someone consciously coins the new term, or it develops through usage and the prevailing assumption that it is already an established word.

Normal word formation is exemplified by nouns such as *inspector,* which is derived from the verb *inspect.* But the verb *edit* comes from *editor,* not—as you might conclude by using the preceding example as a model—the other way around. Other back-formations include *burgle* from *burglar, laze* from *lazy,* and *typewrite* from *typewriter.*

Some back-formations, such as *televise* from *television,* are acceptable English. Others, however, are frowned upon as colloquialisms or jargon, such as *enthuse* from *enthusiasm, liaise* from *liaison,* and *surveille* from *surveillance.*

Because the derived form is usually shorter than the original, back-formation is sometimes classified as a type of abbreviation. Not true. In reality, through derivation, a *new form* of the word is generated, usually a different part of speech.

Now for the so-called "bacronym." Contrary to critics' charges of contrivance (see page 41), it is often impossible to determine with certainty how an acronym was coined. Did the creator begin with the expansion or with the shortened form? Without an earwitness at the scene of coinage, who can say whether the name **A**ccuracy **in** **M**edia, for example, was intentionally chosen for the purpose of creating the acronym **AIM**—or whether the full form, by a happy coincidence, lent itself to the acronym?

So many acronyms today are coined for their similarity to real words that the invention of a plethora of new or borrowed terms to describe them is redundant and unnecessary. For our purposes, a pronounceable abbreviation is an acronym, *whether or not the letters form a "real," meaningful, preexisting word.* (Although we shall contend in the next chapter that meaningful acronyms are esthetically superior to nonsensical "non-word" ones.)

Pronunciation

Some abbreviations may alternatively be pronounced either as initialisms *or* as acronyms. Either form is correct. The **E**qual **R**ights **A**mendment is either **E.R.A.** ("ee-are-ay") or **ERA** (rhymes with Vera). The **s**elf-**a**ddressed **s**tamped **e**nvelope, dreaded by free-lance writers for the rejection slips they often contain, is pronounced either **S.A.S.E.** or "sassy" (sometimes "say-see"). Britain's onerous **VAT** (a 17½ percent **v**alue-**a**dded **t**ax on sales) is pronounced both as an initialism and as an acronym.

Regional variations can create alternative pronunciations. In parts of the Midwest, **U**nited **P**arcel **S**ervice is "ups," not "you-pee-ess," and the **S**cholastic **A**ptitude **T**ests are "sats," not "ess-ay-tees."

Some abbreviations, however, evolve into *one* correct or preferred form, even if the optional pronunciation logically exists.

The popular pejorative **S.O.B.**, for example, is always an initialism, and never a monosyllable suggesting tearfulness. **C.O.D.** is not pronounced like the fish. Astronauts do not report their **E.V.A.** (extravehicular activity) as homophonous with the name of Eva Gabor or Perón. And an **L.E.D.** (**l**ight-**e**mitting **d**iode) is always "el-ee-dee."

Although the presence of the vowels readily allows pronunciation as an acronym, these examples stubbornly resist such treatment.

Why? Who knows? The reasons for linguistic patterns are often elusive. But, as with neckties and other arbitrary social conventions, once a certain form is accepted, it becomes the "right" way.

As we will see in Chapter 6, a corporation or an organization has the prerogative of calling itself whatever it wishes. In some cases, an acronymic pronunciation might sound silly or trivial. This may be why **M.I.T.** and the **D.O.D.** prefer initials. The theatrical union **AFTRA** is an acronym, but the

A.C.L.U. is an initialism, never pronounced "ack-lew." Similarly, **G.O.P.** never rhymes with "top," nor do its conservative sisters in **D.A.R.** utter the name to rhyme with "star." The **W**orld **H**ealth **O**rganization understandably insists that its name is an initialism, not an acronym, and therefore should not be pronounced as a word. ("You work for *who*?")

Abbreviations of Abbreviations

Apparently, acronyms and initialisms are not short enough to satisfy some people. They must be abbreviated still further!

The **A**merican **A**utomobile **A**ssociation is **A.A.A.**, but it is usually vocalized as **Triple-A**, because three consecutive identical letters are difficult to articulate. Similarly, **M**innesota **M**ining and **M**anufacturing doesn't call itself **M.M.M.** but **3M**. The Greek-letter fraternity **Delta Delta Delta** becomes **Tridelt**.

Members of the **A**merican **A**ssociation for the **A**dvancement of **S**cience, or **AAAS**, refer to their professional society as the **Triple-A S** or **A^3S**, the **3** read as "cubed." Similarly, **C^4I** is military jargon for "**C**ommand, **C**ontrol, **C**ommunications, **C**omputers, and **I**ntelligence" (which replaced the earlier **C^3I**, **C^3**, and **C^2**). This technique, however, is a misuse, or perhaps a jest. Strictly speaking, the mathematical functions of squaring, cubing, etc., imply that all the components are identical.

Although such "mega-abbreviations" might sound a bit more mellifluous, they don't necessarily perform the presumably intended function of shortening. Consider Sergeant Bilko's flirtatious "**T.T.F.N.**" for "**T**a-**t**a **f**or **n**ow." The initialism saves no syllables, but made more sense when it served as a radio operator's code; it's still used in computer communications. (In the early 1940s, it was a catchphrase on an English radio show.) And Archie Bunker's "**Double-U Double-U Two**" *increases* the number of syllables—one reason it provoked audience laughter.

A Word from the Critics

Certain scholars and language watchers are not favorably disposed toward the phenomena of acronyms and abbreviations. From legendary linguists to present-day pundits, these guardians of English, often traditional and puristic in their views, denounce what they perceive as the corruption of English by plagues of "initialitis," "alphabet soup," and "agglomerese."

The scores of books and magazine and newspaper articles I collected in my research offer ample evidence of their attitude.

Acronyms are "a menace," said usage expert Wilson Follett, calling them "ambiguous, affected, and at times childish." He even deemed **scuba** (see page 103) an unnecessary coinage, suggesting that the word "gills" be used instead.

Lexicographer Robert Burchfield, in *Unlocking the English Language,* levels his guns against acronyms: "The main disadvantage of such formations is that they are effectively proper names with no power to form derivatives." This means, for example, that a member of **NABET** (**N**ational **A**ssociation of **B**roadcast **E**mployees and **T**echnicians) is *not* called a "Nabeter," and no other forms of the word (such as verb or adjective) exist. "They are barren, in that they cannot generate anything except themselves, and etymologically rootless." (Not quite true, as we'll see in Chapter 4.)

H. L. Mencken, in his classic *The American Language,* thundered against the "monstrosities" of the World War II era, and denounced (in an often-quoted passage) "the characteristic American habit of reducing complex concepts to the starkest abbreviations."

Many critics deplore what they characterize as illegitimate creations. In *Success with Words,* a reference book published by *The Reader's Digest,* Peter Davies condemned "fakes" and "pseudocoinages."

"Honest acronyms emerge, either by pure chance or with a little discreet assistance, from genuine preexisting phrases," said Davies. "Counterfeit acronyms, or retroacronyms, are formed by simply choosing some snappy or appropriate term and devising a phrase to which it can (falsely) be attributed. . . . The backward or cheating approach has now become dangerously common and threatens the integrity of true acronym formation."

Other commentators see acronyms as a symptom of a wider problem: a rash of excessive jargon that is overwhelming civilization. They disapprove of *all* types of abbreviation, especially in medicine, law, government, and the military.

These specialties employ, in their view, an insular "secret language" that obfuscates, euphemizes, and excludes those who are not members of the elite fraternity. Among the pejoratives critics routinely hurl are "gobbledygook," "officialese," "pedagese," "legalese," and "medicant."

"Science is drowning in alphabet soup," charged physics professor Chet Raymo in a *Boston Globe* column. "When acronyms get out of hand, both grace and meaning suffer."

One of the most frequent allegations is the potential for confusion. Some professionals chastise their own colleagues.

"The use of abbreviations on a patient's medical record is rampant—frequently confusing, and sometimes dangerous," warned Kai Haber, a professor of radiology who has cataloged and translated medical terminology.

As for military jargon, Thomas B. Ross, a Defense Department official, told *The New York Times:* "I sometimes think acronyms are an impediment to communication here. I've sat in on budget meetings where the lingo and arcane nature of the subject matter are so complicated I don't think a dozen people in the world could understand what's being discussed."

Shortly after his election as President in 1988, George Bush used the acronym **CASAG** in a media briefing. Puzzled reporters could find no one who was able to explain it. Hours later, a transition team member translated **CASAG:** the **C**abinet **a**nd **S**ub-cabinet **A**dvisory **G**roup that was making recommendations for presidential appointments.

Abbreviations "may become linguistic pests," complained the British linguist Simeon Potter. "These initial letters sometimes baffle us because the writers . . . fail to realize that what is so obvious to them in their own little world may be far from clear to their best-informed readers."

These commentators may gain ammunition from a study conducted by the Department of Journalism of the University of Florida in the early 1960s. The researchers concluded that the average newspaper reader cannot understand one third of the acronyms in headlines.

Acronymic Attempts at Acronym Abolition

In 1908, in a magazine published in England, a letter appeared condemning "the modern lazy habit of substituting initials for names of various organizations or institutions." The writer signed his diatribe "R.B., Upton."

Some critics go so far as to propose a ban on all shortened forms! Over the years, wags have announced the formation of the following (presumably) facetious organizations and movements:

Association for the **A**lleviation of **A**sinine **A**bbreviations and **A**bsurd **A**cronyms (**AAAAAA**)

Committee to **R**esist **A**cronym **P**roliferation (**CRAP**)

Society for the **E**limination of **A**cronyms (**SEA**)

Committee for **H**alting **A**cronymic **O**bliteration of **S**ense (**CHAOS**)

Junk **A**cronyms **W**hen **S**peaking (**JAWS**)

Council to **O**utlaw **C**ontrived and **O**utrageous **A**cronyms (**COCOA**); from a 1977 cartoon in *Punch*

Diminished **R**eliance on **A**cronyms **G**enerally (**DRAG**); coined in a 1977 *New York Times* editorial

At least one such campaign appears to have been more than a jest. In 1974, J. F. Lambertini, Jr., an official of an Iowa university, announced that he was forming a group titled **D**edicated to **E**liminating **A**cronymic **D**esignations, or **DEAD**. He welcomed new members.

Usage authority Theodore M. Bernstein (who, unlike some of his colleagues, had a sense of humor) declared: "**A**cronym **p**roduction, **p**articularly **a**t **l**avish **l**evels, **i**s **n**o **g**ood," which spells **APPALLING**. Professor Raymo proposed forming a **B**oard to **A**ssure **B**asic **E**legance in **L**anguage, or **BABEL**. And during the 1990–91 Persian Gulf War, someone condemned military jargon as **CRASS** ("**c**ryptic **r**eferences, **a**cronyms, **s**lang, **s**horthand").

The recommendations above may not be so farfetched. To prevent dangerous misunderstandings, abbreviations of any kind are prohibited in certain medical and legal documents.

Well! Are acronyms *really* a symptom of the **d**epersonalized **o**vermechanization of **s**ocial **e**nvironments (**DOSE**)? It's clear that **p**undits **a**re **t**ired **o**f **i**llegitimate **s**lang (**PATOIS**). But should we heed lectern lecturers who tell us "**D**o **as** **I** **s**ay!" (**DAIS**)?

Let us now answer the critics.

The Functions and Benefits of Condensed Language

We begin by asking: What is the *purpose* of acronyms—and, more generally, of abbreviations?

Like the remote-control garage-door opener and most of humankind's other inventions, these devices were created to solve problems and fulfill needs. Abbreviations offer us the following advantages:

Brevity and convenience

As linguistic condensation or shorthand, abbreviations are useful in both oral and written communications. They conserve space, effort, and time. They avoid unnecessary repetition. And they usually facilitate communication, rather than obstruct it, as the critics allege.

As a consequence of advances in knowledge and technology, the names of entities, activities, and institutions tend to become long and unwieldy—especially when they must be used repeatedly. Studies have shown that when a word is used more frequently, there is an increased tendency to abbreviate it.

Initialisms and acronyms proliferate in professional fields where concision and/or speed is a priority: telegraphy, stock and commodity trading, medicine, the military services, and even such prosaic settings as short-order restaurants ("**B.L.T.**!"). In these fast-paced, high-pressure occupations, the device of abbreviation evolved as a natural and logical solution to a real problem.

Imagine, for example, having to say *Mohorovičić discontinuity* (the boundary between the earth's crust and the mantle) instead of the terse *Moho.* Or **a**drenocorti**c**o**t**ropic **h**ormone instead of the handier **ACTH**. Or **d**ichloro**d**iphenyl**t**richloroethane for **DDT**. Or, for **DNA**, **d**eoxyribo**n**ucleic **a**cid.

As we shall discover in Chapter 3, abbreviations arose millennia ago to conserve scarce writing materials and the laborious effort of inscribing documents. Today they save space in newspaper headlines, and valuable seconds of time in television newscasts, computer communications, and military and space applications.

Finally, linguists tell us that all language possesses *redundancy*. So repetitive material can often be reduced or eliminated without affecting meaning.

As mnemonic devices

Abbreviations of all sorts serve as memory aids. Acronyms, because they are pronounceable words, make things particularly easy to remember.

You may still recall the colors of the spectrum from a familiar classroom acronym, the mythical personage **ROY G. BIV**. Or the imaginary Indian princess **SOHCAHTOA**, who identified the trigonometric functions. Or the Great Lakes, whose initials spell **HOMES**.

Similarly, to remember the departments of the President's cabinet, students were once instructed to invoke the spirit of **ST. WAPNIACL**, which stood for **S**tate, **T**reasury, and so on. As the cabinet departments changed, however, the mnemonic became obsolete. The fictitious, once-beloved saint has gone to his **g**reat **r**eward **i**n **t**he **s**ky (**GRITS**).

People learning to use firearms are instructed to **BRASS** (**b**reathe, **r**elax, **a**im, **s**queeze, **s**hoot). Members of Alcoholics Anonymous and other twelve-step self-help programs are taught the mnemonic **HALT** (**H**ungry? **A**ngry? **L**onely? **T**ired?) as a way to resist temptation. The coy initialism **X.Y.Z.** is a reminder to e**x**amine **y**our **z**ipper.

In business, **AIDA** is not an opera but the fundamentals of advertising copy: **a**ttention, **i**nterest, **de**sire, **a**ction. **SWOT** means **s**trengths, **w**eaknesses,

opportunities, **t**hreats—factors to consider when marketing a new product.

The six counties of Northern Ireland—**F**ermanagh, **A**rmagh, **T**yrone, **D**erry, **A**ntrim, **D**own—spell the memorable **FATDAD**. (Perhaps it helps the members of the **S**and **L**ake **I**rish **G**atherings **O**rganization, or **SLIGO**, itself the name of an Irish county.)

Medical students use this method to facilitate memorization of vast quantities of technical data. For example, the recommended treatment for a sprained ankle is **r**est, **i**ce, **c**ompression, and **e**levation, or **RICE**.

LEOPARD, coined in 1969 by three doctors named Gorlin, Anderson, and Blaw, represents a syndrome whose symptoms are: **l**entigines, **EKG** changes, **o**cular hypertelorism, **p**ulmonary stenosis, **a**bnormalities of genitalia, **r**etardation of growth, and **d**eafness. In *The Language of Medicine,* John H. Dirckx enthusiastically notes that the device "comes as close to perfection as such a term can, being both an apt metaphor and an acronymic mnemonic" for the first symptom. Lentigines are spots.

Military officer candidates learn the principles of war as **MOSS MOUSE**: **m**aneuver, **o**bjective, **s**ecurity, **s**urprise, **m**ass, **o**ffensive, **u**nity of command, **s**implicity, **e**conomy of force.

Susan Ferraro's *Remembrance of Things Fast* is one of several books that list mnemonics for various purposes and professions. Many are acronyms.

To communicate a message, express a grievance, inspire, and motivate

Some acronyms are loudly tendentious.

When conservative students at Harvard University formed the **A**ssociation **A**gainst **L**earning in the **A**bsence of **R**eligion and **M**orality, they were determined to sound an **AALARM**. On another side of the political spectrum, the **F**eminist **A**nti-**C**ensorship **T**askforce wants everyone to know that its existence is a **FACT**. Meanwhile, the Bucknell University-based **P**artnership **O**f **W**omen **E**ngaged in **R**evolution flaunts its **POWER**.

ASCEND is the **A**dvanced **S**ystem for **C**ommunications and **E**ducation in **N**ational **D**evelopment. **AMIGOS** (unfortunately defunct) stood for **Ame**ricans **M**utually **I**nterested in **G**iving **O**thers a **S**tart. The **S**ystem for **I**ntegrated **M**aintenance and **P**rogram **L**anguage **E**xtension is **SIMPLE. RHYTHM** is **R**emember **H**ow **Y**ou **T**reat **H**azardous **M**aterials (a Du Pont safety program).

Inspirational acronyms include "**S**tart **T**aking **a** **N**ew **D**iscipline," or **STAND**, and "**LIFE**: **L**ive **I**t **F**ully **E**veryday," a T-shirt inscription whose sentiment is superior to its orthography.

Obviously, such coinages are intended to deliver a message via a catchy slogan or battle cry. People with a goal choose a word to express their position or generate a punchy name for their cause, then match it to suitable words to form an acronym. Or the proposed name may just happen to form an appropriate acronym, perhaps with a bit of tweaking.

As noted above, this process is greatly disparaged by critics. Methinks, however, they protest too much! Why is an acronym legitimate if it arises "spontaneously," but somehow illegitimate if it is created by design and deliberation?

The motivations behind the ire of these self-appointed language arbiters are puzzling. After all, many acronyms are creative, witty, on target. They precisely accomplish their intended objective. Who cares if they are "artificial"?

For more organizational, protest, and "cause" acronyms, see Chapter 5. Individuals with gripes sometimes express their displeasure by redefining existing abbreviations in facetious ways. Such satirical acronymy can be extraordinarily ingenious. We'll look at examples in Chapter 8.

To create needed new words

As we've said before, new entities generate the need for new terminology. From computers to space exploration to medicine, all sorts of things abound that were nonexistent just a few years ago.

Acronyms are one way to meet the increasing demand for words. Indeed, because they are coined from the very terms that describe the new entities, this approach has a certain logic and inevitability.

For acronymic words that have entered the English language, and the stories behind them, see Chapter 4. Acronyms created to serve the requirements of various specialized professional fields are discussed in Chapter 6.

As euphemisms

Finally, abbreviations supply a way to disguise taboo words and phrases in (what used to be called) "polite company." The expansion, it is assumed, is implicitly understood by the listener or reader—while remaining safely unintelligible and inoffensive to nearby children and others with sensitive ears.

Euphemistic *initialisms* include **B.S.**, **V.D.**, **B.O.**, **S.O.B.**, and **S.&M.**, expressions such as "Is he **P.O.**'d!," and coy substitutes such as "the **F word**."

The latter form, the substitution of a single initial letter for a word with negative connotations, has migrated to nonsexual areas. In politics, for example, "the **L word**" is **l**iberal, "the **R word**" is **r**ecession, and "the **T word**" is **t**axes.

Euphemistic *acronyms* are less common. One is **snafu**—which has become part of the language, and which we shall examine in detail later.

Opponents and Defenders: In Search of a Balance

The many benefits and advantages of abbreviation have been neatly summarized by Ralph Slovenko, professor of law and psychiatry at Detroit's Wayne State University Law School—and a fellow acronym enthusiast. In an article in *The Journal of Psychiatry and Law,* Professor Slovenko wrote:

"Expansive technology, science, bureaucracy, and

organizational activity have all combined to put a strain on our language. They have introduced into the language many long, hard-to-remember, or hard-to-pronounce words. To manage, people have turned to abbreviated language—initialisms and acronyms."

He's right. In light of the benefits of abbreviation, then, should we not celebrate rather than bemoan these handy devices?

We certainly think so. But what about all those critics we heard from earlier? They deserve a reply, and here it is.

In *The Language of Medicine,* John H. Dirckx answers, with justifiable testiness, the "pedants and busybodies" who ridicule medical terminology.

"Every professional or trade jargon seems obscure and bizarre to outsiders," observes Dr. Dirckx. "Why should informal speech and writing be held to the standards of formal speech and writing, or professional jargon to the canons of general language? A system of communication that transmits messages clearly and effectively among those who use it serves its function adequately."

As even most of the carpers would agree, language is (metaphorically speaking) a living organism, in a continuous state of evolution. New words arise in many ways. One such method is abbreviation. Novel terms enrich the language and enhance our ability to communicate, progress, and prosper, both as individuals and as a society.

Sure, the results may at times be infelicitous. But

neologisms, like species, flourish or perish according to the law of natural selection.

The charge of exclusion and secrecy also seems exaggerated. If members of an in-group *really* wanted to keep things private, they would not use letter abbreviations, which are often transparent and quickly decoded by laypeople. Espionage agencies, which employ syllabic acronyms such as **COINTELPRO** and **COMINFIL**, and cultish fraternal groups that boast pompous titles such as **G.H.P. & P.** ("**G**rand **H**igh **P**riest and **P**rophet"), are hardly keeping things on the **Q.T.**!

The apocalyptic bemoaning of the critics, then, is surely overblown. But they do score some valid points. Abbreviation, when excessive or misused, can subvert the very purposes it intends to serve, and obfuscate instead of clarify communication. If the recipient of a message, either oral or written, does not understand the expansion or the meaning of an abbreviation, the consequences can be delay or disaster.

Another source of confusion stems from an inescapable fact of reality: Many initialisms and acronyms have *multiple* expansions. Or, as linguists say, an abbreviation can be *polysemic.* For acronyms, this situation is unavoidable, as only a finite number of pronounceable letter combinations exists.

In clinical medicine, for example, **PAS** or **P.A.S.** can mean either **p**eripheral **a**nterior **s**ynechia, or **p**ersistent **a**trial **s**tandstill, or **p**ulmonary **a**rterial **s**tenosis, or even **p**atient **a**ppointments and **s**cheduling. If you are on your way to surgery, the meaning could matter!

STOP is **S**ecurity **T**racking of **O**ffice **P**roperty, a system to protect business computers from theft. But **STOP** is also **S**ave **t**he **O**ppressed **P**eople (an organization that attempted to end U.S. trade with the Soviet Union in Cold War days), and **S**ociety **T**hat **O**pposes **P**ornography, and **S**oftware **T**heft **O**pposition **P**roject. Not to mention groups wanting to **STOP**: **t**he **O**cean **P**ollution . . . **t**he **O**il **P**rofiteers . . . **t**he **O**lympic **P**rison . . . **T**axation **o**f **P**ublications.

HELP is **H**elp **E**stablish **L**asting **P**eace, **H**omeless **E**mergency **L**iaison **P**roject, **H**ousing **E**nterprise for the **L**ess **P**rivileged, **H**arlem **E**astside **L**ifesaving **P**rogram, and others.

PAL is the **P**olice **A**thletic **L**eague, but it acronymically represents at least fifty-three other things. **SCOPE** has seventeen meanings; **ADAPT** has eleven. Positive-sounding words such as **PRIDE** and **ORACLE** are appropriated by many groups.

In *The Wall Street Journal,* a letter writer testily complained about an editorial that truncated the terrorist group **R**ed **A**rmy **F**action (in German, *Rote Armee Fraktion*) to **RAF**. The irate reader sternly admonished the editors: " '**RAF**' has meant and *always* will mean '**R**oyal **A**ir **F**orce.' " As Gilda Radner used to say, "That's very different!"

Herewith a cautionary tale, probably apocryphal, of the dangers of abbreviation (or perhaps illiteracy). A farmer shot a migratory bird. When he retrieved his quarry, he discovered a tag that read "Wash. Biol. Surv." (short for Washington Biological Survey). The next day, he penned an angry complaint: "My wife followed the cooking instructions on the leg tag and I want to tell you it was horrible!"

The accusation that multiple expansions and alternative meanings cause problems is not without merit. But as with language in general, *context* usually provides clues to meaning.

The critics seem to forget that many *non*-abbreviated words can be misinterpreted or not understood. Numerous words possess two or more senses, providing fertile territory for bafflement and snafus.

For example, the homophones *oral* and *aural* are frequently misheard and misconstrued. Other candidates for confusion: *counsel* and *council, died* and *dyed, right* and *write.* Yet no one contends that the problem should be solved by abolishing the words!

The Solution to Confusion, or: Acronym Etiquette

A few simple measures can help minimize confusion and enhance clarity in both written and spoken communications.

When using an acronym, or *any* abbreviation, bear in mind that the reader or listener may not know what it means, or may interpret it incorrectly. Observe the following ***R**ules **o**f **A**cronym **R**espect* (or **ROAR** for short).

First, say the authors of the usage guide *Modern*

English, "the *needless* abbreviation of words is a form of discourtesy to the reader and should be avoided" (emphasis added).

When you have good reason to use an unfamiliar initialism or acronym, either in conversation or in writing, provide the full form at the first mention, along with a definition or explanation if necessary (a process called *glossing*). You may then use the abbreviated form with impunity.

An effective and accepted style is as follows:

First mention:

Greatest **L**overs **o**f **A**ll **T**ime (**GLOAT**) will hold its annual meeting on Thursday at 8 P.M. in the Community Center auditorium. . . .

Subsequent mentions:

Founded in 1993, **GLOAT** is an elite organization whose members must document their achievements in order to be admitted. . . .

This method works well—until later on when the listener or reader forgets the expansion! So don't overload. And, when necessary, repeat the full form.

Unfortunately, the authors of some usage and style guides advise *against* this commonsense procedure, counseling instead to avoid abbreviations completely! But we suspect that these people are not living in the real world.

Are Acronyms Puns?

Because a *meaningful* acronym creates an ambiguous or double sense—the real word and the new coinage—some people classify acronyms as a species of pun.

For example, **CAVEAT** means warning *and* "**C**ode **a**nd **V**isual **E**ntry **A**uthorization **T**echnique." I enjoy coining brand-new acronyms from familiar phrases, such as **TAPAS** (**T**here's **a** **p**rinciple **a**t **s**take), **WASP** (**W**hat **a** **s**well **p**arty!), and **NANNY** (**N**ot **a** **n**ative **N**ew **Y**orker).

So are acronyms puns? Yes and no.

Joel Sherzer, a professor of anthropology at the University of Texas, Austin, defines *pun* as "a form of speech play in which a word or phrase unexpectedly and simultaneously combines two unrelated meanings." Strictly speaking, a pun is the humorous use of a *homonym* (same sound and spelling, but different meanings—e.g., *cast* of a play, *cast* for a leg) or a *homophone* (same sound but a different spelling—e.g., *bread* and *bred*). Dictionaries, however, don't always agree on the precise definitions of these and related terms. They are frequently used inexactly and interchangeably.

Often, *any* pairing of words with similar sounds is loosely termed a pun—although *paronomasia* (from Greek, meaning "a slight change in name") is in such cases the more accurate term. *Wordplay* is an even wider rubric.

Acronym creation certainly involves wordplay,

but the process may be closer to anagrams, Scrabble, and other alphabet games than to punnery.

To coin an acronym, and then announce that it's a pun, strikes me as a bit presumptuous. Once an acronym is established and accepted, however, this argument becomes stronger—for instance, if a journalist refers to the leaders of the **C**ongress **o**f **R**acial **E**quality as "the core of **CORE**."

And acronyms *do* lend themselves irresistibly to punning references. For example, Apple Computer's 1992 venture into the burgeoning field of **p**ersonal **i**nteractive **e**lectronics was masterminded by a unit of the company called (what else?) Apple **PIE**. An educational cable television network, **M**ind **E**xtension **U**niversity, boasts the call letters **ME/U**. And **SALT**, the arms negotiations, inspired among headline writers a flood of saline puns.

Also in the spirit of wordplay are humorous reinterpretations and redefinitions of acronyms and initialisms, which you'll find in Chapter 8, among other places. Games that play on the sounds of letters, mentioned briefly above, are explained more fully in Chapter 9.

We conclude this chapter with the observation that acronyms are a species *superior* to initialisms and other forms of abbreviation. While initialisms are just random bunches of letters, acronyms require originality and creative thought. The remaining pages of this book will, I hope, help to prove this contention.

CHAPTER 2

❖

Principles And Rules, Acronymic Design, Ingenious Grading Methodology (PARADIGM)

Humankind has long been puzzled by deep, metaphysical questions concerning the nature of acronyms and their place in the universe.

What are the rules for the proper formation of acronyms? How are they created? How does one distinguish a *good* coinage from a *bad* one?

Here at last are the definitive answers.

How does one go about coining an acronym?

You might begin with a list of the key components desired in the full form. Often, the initial letters create something close to a word—but not quite. You then scramble or delete or add one or more letters, choosing words to fit, until the perfect acronym emerges.

For this task, Scrabble tiles are useful tools. Some

personal computer programs (such as Namer, from the Salinon Corporation, Dallas) automatically generate permutations of letters and words.

In a presentation at a 1984 conference in Barcelona, titled "Humour and Invention in the Coining and Use of Acronyms," Félix Rodríguez González, a Spanish linguist, said: "One may proceed in various ways: manipulating the syntax of the acronym's underlying phrase; eliminating an initial; or else representing a word of the original phrase with a letter, syllable, or segment of a word, whichever is most convenient."

Must an acronym be a *real* word, or is *any* pronounceable combination of letters acceptable?

Glad you asked.

The newly created locution may be either a meaningless and nonexistent "word" *or* a genuine, meaningful, preexisting word.

Pronounceable but meaningless coinages include **OPEC** (**O**rganization of **P**etroleum **E**xporting **C**ountries), **OSHA** (**O**ccupational **S**afety and **H**ealth **A**dministration), **DARPA** (**D**efense **A**dvanced **R**esearch **P**rojects **A**gency), and **NORC** (**n**aturally **o**ccurring **r**etirement **c**ommunity). Well, we can't say the last one is totally senseless; in Australia, *nork* is a slang term for breast—though more popular in the 60s than today.

Some acronyms are not only meaningless but

also cumbersome, such as the trade unions **ILGWU** (**I**nternational **L**adies' **G**arment **W**orkers' **U**nion) and **IATSE** (**I**nternational **A**lliance of **T**heatrical **S**tage **E**mployees), which are often pronounced "ill-gwoo" and "eye-OTT-see."

Of course, an acronymic coinage is often a real word, but one that is irrelevant or inappropriate to the purpose at hand. For example, no logical reason exists for a **c**ost **o**f **l**iving **a**djustment to be a **COLA.** Or for **p**ersons **i**n **n**eed of **s**upervision (formerly known as juvenile delinquents) to be called **PINS**. Or for the **D**efense **I**ndustrial **S**ecurity **C**learance **O**ffice to be **DISCO**.

Examples of acronyms that are both meaningful and appropriate to their purposes include **ALERT** (**Al**cohol **L**evel **E**valuation **R**oadside **T**ester), **DREAM** (**D**esign **R**ealization, **E**valuation, **a**nd **M**odeling), **PROMPT** (**P**roduction **R**eviewing, **O**rganizing, and **M**onitoring of **P**erformance **T**echniques), and the **ZIP** (**Z**one **I**mprovement **P**lan) Code, which zippily speeds—presumably—all of our letters to their destinations.

Or consider **FANS** (**F**ranchise of **A**mericans **N**eeding **S**ports), Saskatchewan's **PLEA** (**P**ublic **Le**gal **E**ducation **A**ssociation), and **HOG** (**H**arley **O**wner's **G**roup), which puns on a slang expression for motorcycle. Regrettably, however, **FLIC** (the **F**ilm **L**ibrary **I**nformation **C**ouncil) was merged into the Educational Film Library Association.

Two aptly named British crime-fighting programs are **MASTIFF** (**M**odular **A**utomated **S**ystem **t**o

Identify **F**riend from **F**oe) and **TIGER** (**T**errorist **I**ntelligence **G**athering **E**valuation and **R**eview).

Meaningful and appropriate acronyms that are longer, and hence more clever and impressive, include: **EMPHASIS** (**E**valuation **M**anagement using **P**ast **H**istory **A**nalysis for **S**cientific **I**nventory **S**imulation), **MAESTRO** (**M**achine-**A**ssisted **E**ducational **S**ystem for **T**eaching by **R**emote **O**peration), and the United Kingdom's **FREDERICK** (**F**amily **R**obot for **E**ntertainment, **D**iscussion and **E**ducation, **R**etrieval of **I**nformation, and **C**ollation of **K**nowledge).

Either type of acronym, meaningful or meaningless, is acceptable. But as these examples demonstrate, acronyms that form genuine words are more elegant and hence superior. When the coinage is relevant and apropos, we have reached the apex of the art.

In such cases, the acronym is, as linguists say, "related to its lexical meaning." Professor Rodríguez notes that when such acronyms are "deliberately composed through homonymy," they possess "connotative, denotative, or mnemonic values."

Commentators have variously named such specimens "apposite acronyms," "prefabricated acronyms," "punning acronyms," "reverse acronyms," and "lexical context acronyms." (Not to mention "bacronyms," a term earlier discussed—and dismissed.)

The *best* examples of the art might be called *quality acronyms*. For additional evaluative criteria, please see below and refer to the definitive ranking system at the end of this chapter. Our awards for the best specimens are presented in Chapter 10.

Are "small" words, such as conjunctions and prepositions, properly included in the acronym —or should they be skipped?

Either route is acceptable, but observe the principle of *consistency.* Ideally, your coinage should incorporate *all* the "small" words or *none* of them. For a quality acronym, you can't have it both ways—although some novice neologists try to get away with it.

Consider for example, **A S**ociety **t**o **H**elp the **M**orale of **A**sthmatics, or **ASTHMA.** Clever, but how can we explain the inclusion of "a" and "to," while "the" and "of" are omitted? Clearly, some fudging was done. Ditto for **FLAME** (**F**oundation of **L**ight **a**nd **M**etaphysical **E**ducation) and **WARPATH** (**W**orld **A**ssociation to **R**emove **P**rejudice **A**gainst **t**he **H**andicapped).

Virtually every word in the English language contains one or more *vowels,* which make words pronounceable. By a happy coincidence, many "small" connective words begin with vowels: *a, an, and, as, at, in, is, it, of, on, or.* These are called *function words* or *particles.* Such prepositions, conjunctions, and indefinite articles serve as valuable tools in the process of acronym formation.

An acronym that *incorporates* the initial letters of *all* the small words, instead of skipping all of them, is stylistically more elegant and comes closer to achieving acronymic perfection.

What other rules govern the proper construction of an acronym?

The expansion (full phrase) should ideally contain *all* the initial letters of the acronym—and *only* those letters.

The best acronyms employ *no fewer* letters than the initial letters of the words in the expansion—and *no more.* Extraneous letters—those *not* among the initial letters in the expansion—are prohibited.

Some (imperfect) acronyms "cheat" by, for example, arbitarily using *more than one* letter from the same word—or by cavalierly *omitting* some initial letters of major words.

Our point can be demonstrated by a few examples:

Employees of New York's Museum of Modern Art formed the **P**rofessional and **A**dministrative **St**aff **A**ssociation (**PASTA**). Whether or not these aesthetic folks share a passion for Italian food, they cheated by borrowing the extra (noninitial) letter.

Similarly, **CLEAR-TV** is an awkward coinage that supposedly means "**C**hristian **Lea**ders for **R**esponsible **T**ele**v**ision." But the concerned clergymen may still achieve salvation. They could solve their problem by redefining the organization's name to mean (perhaps) "**C**hristian **L**eaders **E**nthusiastic **A**bout . . ." We pray that they will mend their ways!

Except for insertion of the extraneous letter, **CONDUCT**—for **C**ommittee **on** **D**ecent, **U**nbiased **C**ampaign **T**actics—would qualify as rather neat.

Some groups omit from their names a major initial letter in the expansion. The **N**ational **O**rganization to **I**nsure a **S**ound-controlled **E**nvironment shouts that its acronym is **NOISE**, getting away with it by hyphenating. Ditto for **P**arents **o**f **S**urrogate-borne **I**nfants and **T**oddlers **i**n **V**erbal **E**xchange, or **POSITIVE**. Meanwhile, **SPACE** claims it is the **S**ociety for **P**rivate **a**nd **C**ommercial **E**arth Stations. Hmmm . . . guess they figured SPACES would not communicate their mission as dramatically. And a Connecticut social service organization, **B**etter **O**verall **O**utcome through **S**tudent and Family **T**raining, insists on calling itself "Project **Boost**," apparently unconcerned that the family is unrepresented in its acronym.

The **E**u**r**opean Community **A**ction **S**cheme for the **M**obility of **U**niversity **S**tudents, or **ERASMUS** (an ambitious educational program providing grants for study in member countries), is superficially clever. Erasmus was a famous sixteenth-century Renaissance scholar. But the **R** is evidently—and illegally—borrowed from the interior of European, while the **C** of **C**ommunity is blithely ignored.

"Creative misspelling" is also a no-no. Consider these shameless offenders:

CARISMA, **C**omputer-**A**ided **R**esearch **i**nto **S**tock **M**arket **A**pplications

RAINBO, **R**esearch **a**nd **I**nstrumentation for **Na**tional **B**ioscience **O**perations

CORECT (which isn't!), **C**itizens **O**rganized to **R**estore an **E**ffective **C**orporate **T**ax

CHECMATE, **C**ompact **H**igh-**E**nergy **C**apacitor **M**odule **A**dvanced **T**echnology **E**xperiment

To produce a meaningful acronym, some folks really push it, employing clumsy syntax or inserting extraneous or redundant elements. Consider these contrived and tautological efforts:

IMPRINT, for **I**mproved **M**edical **P**rograms and **R**eadiness **I**mmediately, **N**ot **T**omorrow (of the Retired Officers Association); **TRACY**, for **T**echnical **R**eports **A**utomated **C**ataloging—**Y**es (a project of the National Oceanic and Atmospheric Administration); the United Kingdom's **FEASIBLE**, for **F**inite **E**lement **A**nalysis **S**ensibly **I**mplemented **b**y **L**east **E**ffort; and **SCRIMP**, meaning **S**ave **C**ash, **R**educe **I**mmediately **M**eat **P**rices (a 1963 consumer protest in Boston).

We must note a few exceptions, however, to our all-and-only-the-initial-letters-in-the-word rule.

Because almost every English word starting with Q follows with a U, we may regard QU as a single character for acronymic purposes. Thus, an acronym may legitimately incorporate *both* letters even though the expansion contains no word beginning with U. Examples: **QUBIC**, for **Qu**ery **b**y **I**mage **C**ontent (a computer graphics program), and the clever **TORQUE**, for **T**ruck **O**perators' **R**oad **Qu**alifying **E**xam.

Similarly, the use of X for the homophonous affix "ex" is permissible, as in **PHOENIX**, for **P**lasma **H**eating **O**btained by **E**nergetic **N**eutral **I**njection E**x**periment.

The **WELL**, a popular California-based computer network, is an acronym for **W**hole **E**arth '**L**ectronic **L**ink. This slangy clipping might at first appear to violate our rules. But we'll grade it as legitimate because the character of the network and its users (young, antiestablishment types) is eminently compatible with the colloquial truncation. In any case, we can hardly disapprove of an abbreviation within an acronym!

Finally, as noted in the previous chapter, the syllabic acronym is legitimate—but *only* if the result employs the initial syllables *consistently*. A syllabic acronym must be *totally* syllabic. It's unacceptable to attempt to have it both ways—mixing initials and syllables—within the same acronym.

Violators of this rule include **Aslib**, the **A**ssociation of **S**cientific **Lib**raries; **BITNET**, for **B**ecause **I**t's **T**ime **Net**work (a university computer link); and the alloy **Nitinol** (named for the chemical symbols for **ni**ckel and **ti**tanium, and the **N**aval **O**rdnance **L**aboratory, where it was created).

In written communications, what are the rules on style and punctuation? First, should *periods* be used in acronyms?

No. Period! Because acronyms are pronounced as words, periods ("full stops" if you're British, "points" if you're a lexicographer) are superfluous.

But periods *should* be used for *initialisms,* to indicate that the individual letters are sounded out. Examples: **P.S.**, **F.Y.I.**, **I.R.S.** Despite their vowels, **P.O.W.** and **M.I.A.** are initialisms, not acronyms, and the periods help communicate that fact. Pronouncing these two terms as acronyms would sound flippant and insensitive.

Yet despite these commonsense rules, many proprietors of initialisms customarily *drop* the periods. Why? One argument is that omitting punctuation looks cleaner and more modern. For examples of this phenomenon from the business world, see Chapter 6, page 158.

Conversely, some acronyms are (incorrectly) written and printed *with* periods. This error is especially prevalent in "clever" titles of movies and television shows. See Chapter 6, page 180.

In this book, our style is periods for initialisms and *no* periods for acronyms—except where we respect the explicit preference of an organization or institution. **Boldfacing** is employed for emphasis only.

We suppose it's futile to resist those who insist on

anomalous renderings of their names, such as Toys "Я" Us. But such eccentric typography can cause problems.

In a major newspaper, the television series ***M*A*S*H*** was printed as ***MAAASAH***—which sounds more like a miniseries set in the Old South and starring Ed Asner. Evidently, the typesetter misread each asterisk as if it were the letter "A."

In 1990, the two founders of a New York City bakery decided to call their establishment **S. T.** Famous Bread, using the initials of their first names. But customers thought the name meant "**St.** Famous." The owners decided not to fight the inevitable, so now the store is officially St. Famous Bread, Inc. But I was probably not the only customer to experience difficulty locating the number in the phone book and from Directory Assistance.

Are acronyms properly spelled with all upper-case (capital) letters or with all lower-case letters? Or should they begin with an initial cap, followed by small letters? Help!

You're not alone. Like the origin of the universe, this is a complex and baffling question.

When an acronym is first coined, it should be written with ALL UPPER-CASE letters. That way, it can readily be identified as an abbreviation and—if it is spelled the same way as a genuine word—differentiated from its "normal" counterpart. For example, we know that **APPLE** is the **A**ssociation of **P**ublic and **P**rivate **L**abor **E**mployees and not the fruit, and that **WORM** is a computer term for **w**rite **o**nce, **r**ead **m**any, and not the vermicular creature inhabiting the aforementioned pomaceous victual.

Of course, some acronyms ultimately enter the language and become legitimate, everyday words. When this happens, they are transformed into lower-case. For examples of this phenomenon, turn to Chapter 4.

Acronymic names of organizations and companies are usually all caps, although some groups, as noted above, have their own quirky styles and prefer initial cap/lower-case.

According to William Safire, "when an acronym exceeds four letters, capitalize only the first letter." Thus, **SALT** (**S**trategic **A**rms **L**imitation **T**alks) is all caps, while **Start** (**St**rategic **A**rms **R**eduction **T**alks) should be initial-capped only.

Although I enjoy Mr. Safire's columns, I disagree with him on this point. (On another occasion, his standard was "more than three letters.") No logical basis appears to support his rule—and it could cause trouble. As Ralph Slovenko asks: "Without all caps, how would the term be recognized as an acronym rather than as simply a word?" Even with the initial cap, **Start** might be misread as the "start" of the negotiations. The all-upper-case rule helps to avoid this problem.

Only if and when an acronym enters the language as a "true" word (determined by usage and the anguished deliberations of lexicographers) does it properly become lower-cased.

It might be nice if words such as **radar** could indefinitely retain their all-caps orthography. That form would serve as a reminder of, and tribute to, their acronymic origins. But at times we must bow to convention.

Is it permissible for an acronym to be a word that's in the expansion?

This practice appears to be in vogue, apparently because some coiners regard the device as clever.

The acronym is often the *first* word of the full form. The **D**og **O**wners' **G**uild is **DOG**. **C**hefs **H**elping to **E**nhance **F**ood **S**afety is **CHEFS**. The **B**ass **A**nglers **S**portsman **S**ociety is **BASS**. **H**air **A**wareness **I**nformation and **R**esearch is **HAIR**. The **F**arm **A**udience **R**esearch **M**easurement **S**ervice is **FARMS.**

Sometimes the acronym is a fragment of a word in the expansion, such as **DOC**, for **D**octors **O**ught to **C**are (a public health education group); **FAIR**, for **F**airness and **A**ccuracy **i**n **R**eporting; and **OCEAN**, for **O**ceanographic **C**oordination **E**valuation **An**alysis **N**etwork.

Frankly, these specimens strike me as uncreative and redundant. A "quality acronym" is invariably an entirely *new* word.

Do other kinds of illegitimate acronyms exist?

You'd better believe it!

Some misguided folks try to *force* a nonexistent acronym from a series of mere initials.

On college campuses, students casually refer to the **R**eserve **O**fficers **T**raining **C**orps, **R.O.T.C.**, as "rot-see." **S**atellite **M**aster **A**ntenna **T**ele**v**ision, **S.M.A.T.V.**, is pronounced "smat-vee." And on Wall Street, **S.I.P.C.**, the **S**ecurities **I**nvestor **P**rotection **C**orporation, is called "sipick."

In the 1960s, the **S**tudent **N**onviolent (later **N**ational) **C**oordinating **C**ommittee, **S.N.C.C.**, was referred to as "snick." Surgeons say "cabbage" for **C.A.B.G.**, a **c**oronary **a**rtery **b**ypass **g**raft. And **S.C.S.I.**, a **s**mall **c**omputer **s**ystems **i**nterface, becomes the unprepossessing "scuzzy."

This type of violation is especially prevalent in government agencies and the military. For instance:

> The **F**ederal **H**ome **L**oan **B**ank **B**oard, or **F.H.L.B.B.**, a short-lived federal regulatory agency, was pronounced by industry people as "flub-bub."
>
> The **R**esource **C**onservation and **R**ecovery **A**ct, **R.C.R.A.** (a federal law governing the handling and disposal of hazardous waste), is pronounced "RICK-ra."

In 1983, President Reagan created the **S**enior **A**rms **C**ontrol **P**olicy **G**roup, **S.A.C.P.G.**, which became "sack-pig."

To Pentagon personnel, a **S**ea-**L**aunched **C**ruise **M**issile, or **S.L.C.M.**, is "slickem." **N**ational **S**ecurity **S**tudy **M**emorandums, or **N.S.S.M.**s, are "nissims."

The military's **Humvee** is from the attempted pronunciation of **H.M.M.W.V.** (a **h**igh-**m**obility, **m**ultipurpose, **w**heeled **v**ehicle, a combination Jeep and light truck); and **Huff Duff** is from **H.F.D.F.**, **H**igh-**F**requency **D**irection **F**inding.

Good grief! All these specimens are mere initialisms masquerading as acronyms. They are "pronounceable" only because the speaker inserts extraneous vowels. In some cases, one of the letters is pronounced phonetically (e.g., "vee" for V). Where that happens, these examples resemble the hybrid form (exemplified by **VTOL**), which was discussed in the previous chapter.

These pseudo-acronymic constructions should be equipped with periods (often they are not) and pronounced letter by letter, as any self-respecting initialism should. We hereby ban (mostly) such charlatans from our pages.

Beware of impostors. Know your acronyms, keep your standards high, and accept no substitutes.

Introducing the AHA Rating Scale

As with any art form, one can find both good and bad works. Some acronyms are appropriate, felicitous, graceful, and witty. Others are awkward, strained, and bogus.

"We need a way to evaluate the quality of acronyms!" you're probably shouting.

Now such a tool exists. I call it the "**A**scending **H**ierarchy of **A**cronyms," or **AHA** for short. Appropriately, this system employs letter grades. Here is the scale, from lowest to highest, with examples:

UNGRADED — Initialisms and other non-acronyms. **C.I.A.**, **T.G.I.F.**, **A.S.P.C.A.**

F — "Pseudo-acronyms" that torture a mere initialism into semi-pronounceable form, such as "Fannie Mae" from **F.N.M.A.**, the **F**ederal **N**ational **M**ortgage **A**ssociation, or **P.F.I.A.B.**, pronounced "piffiab," the **P**resident's **F**oreign **I**ntelligence **A**dvisory **B**oard.

D — Contrived, labored, or misspelled formations. **SLOWPOKE** (**S**afe **Low**-**Po**wer **C**ritical **E**xperiment), a nuclear energy project.

C — Meaningless "non-word" acronyms. Pronounceable, but *not* genuine English words. **EPCOT, NASA, OPEC, SEATO.**

B– Imperfect acronyms. These violators skip letters, insert extraneous ones, or mix syllables and letters. **FOCUS**, for **F**ellowship **o**f **C**hristians in **U**niversities and **S**chools, and **TRAVEL**, for **Tra**nsportable **V**ertical **E**rectable **L**auncher.

B *Real* words, but which are *not* particularly relevant to their purposes. **CAFE**, for **c**orporate **a**verage **f**uel **e**conomy; **MAMBO**, for **M**editerranean **A**ssociation of **M**arine **B**iology and **O**ceanography; **CAVALCADE**, for **c**alibrating, **am**plitude-**v**ariation, **a**nd **l**evel-**c**orrecting **a**nalog-**d**igital **e**quipment.

A to A+ The highest-quality acronyms. Coinages, and their corresponding expansions, that are meaningful, apt, and clever. **ALERT**, for **A**merican **L**ifesaving **E**mergency **R**esponse **T**eam; **MOO**, for **M**ilkbottles **O**nly **O**rganization.

For the verdict on the best acronyms of all, see Chapter 10. In the meantime, I have appointed myself the chief judge of acronymic perfection. Court is now in session.

CHAPTER 3

❖

Short History Of Abbreviation, Lore, Scholarship (SHOALS)

According to some accounts, the acronyms of the World War I or II periods were the earliest ever created.

Erroneous and absurd! Acronyms boast a long and proud history of thousands of years.

When was the *first* acronym devised? It's hard to say (unlike acronyms themselves, which are usually easy to say). As with many great events, the precise origins of acronymy are lost in the pages of time. But we can hazard some intelligent speculations. This chapter presents an abbreviated (ahem!) history of the phenomenon.

In the Beginning

"The tendency to compress is as old as language itself," observed Bill Bryson in *The Mother Tongue.*

He's not kidding. Joseph T. Shipley's *In Praise of*

English tells us that "abbreviations were first employed in Sumerian, the earliest recorded language." The Sumerians lived in Mesopotamia in the third millennium B.C.E. They employed a *pictographic* or *ideographic* system of writing, in which each sign represents an object or concept.

"Alphabetic writing first surfaced in the Sinai and Canaan in the first half of the second millennium B.C.," says Robert K. Logan in *The Alphabet Effect*. A Semitic people who, according to one popular hypothesis, worked as slaves in copper and turquoise mines for the Egyptians, borrowed from their bosses the notion of an alphabet based on sounds. While it contained the germ of the alphabetic principle, however, the Egyptian hieroglyphic system, like the Sumerian language, was overwhelmingly ideographic.

But here is the part that is of greatest interest to us. Logan explains that the signs in this early alphabet "operate according to a phonetic acrostic principle whereby each sign represents an object and the sound value of the sign is the same as the first consonant of the name of the object depicted. Words are spelled out phonetically using the names acrostically. For example [to use an English-language analogy], **cat** would be spelled by picturing a **c**an, an **a**pple, and a **t**able in sequence."

Thus acronyms (of a sort) were present at the very birth of the alphabet and phonetic writing!

Archaeologists digging in the Sinai Peninsula in 1905 found inscriptions of the type just described, which exemplify what is called *acrophony* ("initial sound"). Many scholars believe that these inscriptions (variously dated between 1850 and 1475 B.C.E.) constitute the earliest evidence of alphabetic writing.

We should note that many hypotheses on the origins of written language have been advanced, some conflicting. At least five distinct peoples and every country around the eastern Mediterranean have been credited with the invention of the alphabet. The full story is shrouded in the sands (perhaps literally as well as metaphorically) of time.

But most experts agree that the acrophonic principle was critical to the creation and evolution of the alphabet. From these humble beginnings came the letters, syllables, and words that constitute written phonetic language as we know it.

The Acrostic

The ancestor of the modern acronym is the *acrostic*. In the analogy just discussed, "CAT" can be called an acrostic. But the term also refers to a prose or verse composition in which a word or phrase, or the alphabet in sequence, is created by the first letter of each line.

Acrostics that spell out a name or a sentence were composed in ancient Babylonia. Seven examples have survived, two of which can be dated precisely to the seventh century B.C.E.; another may be as old as 1000 B.C.E. One Babylonian acrostic, a hymn to a popular deity of the day, spells out his name: "God Nabû." The others, with one exception, are also hymns or prayers, two of them commissioned by kings.

If you can read the original Hebrew, you'll find in the Old Testament a type of acrostic called an *abecedarian.* In Psalms 25 and 34, for example, the first line begins with *Aleph,* the second with *Beth,* and so on through the entire Hebrew alphabet. The device is also used in Psalm 119, but in this case each line within each stanza begins with the same letter. The twenty-two stanzas thus use all twenty-two letters of the Hebrew alphabet.

Depending on the interpretation of fragmentary evidence, the Old Testament contains a total of either fourteen or fifteen acrostics. No word or sentence acrostics have been identified with certainty, despite the speculations of some biblical scholars.

Acrostics were also composed in ancient Greece and Rome. As just one of many examples, the arguments (summaries or prefaces) of the comedies of the Roman playwright Plautus (c. 254–184 B.C.E.) spelled out the titles of his plays.

Why were acrostics composed? They functioned as mnemonic devices, facilitating the oral transmission of important works. Sometimes they identified the author, or the individual (often a patron or loved one) who was addressed. Some experts suggest that the restrictions of the form posed a deliberate literary challenge to the writer, much as a sonnet does. Finally, acrostics had religious and mystical functions. The alphabetic acrostics of the Old Testament may have symbolized totality or completeness, much as we indicate the idea of "all of it" with the phrase "from A to Z."

William Michael Soll, writing in the journal *Biblica,* notes that because one begins reading an acrostic in the customary horizontal fashion, "the impression of the finished product is the reverse of the process of composition: the poem gives the appearance of generating the acrostic, as if revealing a secret about itself."

Although sometimes criticized as artificial, this venerable literary tradition continued—through the Middle Ages, the Renaissance, and the Elizabethan era. Several great poets indulged in the form. Acrostics are usually serious, but they can also be playful. More on the latter function in Chapter 9.

The Post-Biblical Period

Acronyms as we know them may have originated in Jewish literature.

The Hebrew name for the Old Testament is ***T****anakh*, a word created from ***T****orah,* ***N****eviim,* and ***K****etuvim,* or Pentateuch, Prophets, and Hagiographica, its three books. (These English transliterations do not precisely match the acronym because Hebrew has no written vowels. When written Hebrew is spoken, vowels are interpolated, based on the context or diacritical marks.)

To observant Jews back then, and to this day, the

name of God was considered so sacred that it was never pronounced. In writing, it was rendered as **YHVH**, a device called the *Tetragrammaton* (from Greek meaning "four letters"). With the interpolation of vowels, these characters were read as **Yahweh** or **Jehovah**.

According to legend, Judas Maccabeus, the Jewish military hero of the second century B.C.E., took his surname from an acrostic—or acronym. He chose a verse from Exodus as his slogan and placed the Hebrew initial letters of the passage on his banners before marching into battle. After emerging victorious, his soldiers called him **Maccabeus**, the word the letters spelled.

The everyday use of initialisms also began quite a while ago. In *Our Language,* Simeon Potter remarked: "The Romans wrote **A.U.C.** (***A**nno **u**rbis **c**onditae*) and **S.P.Q.R.** (***S**enatus **p**opulus**q**ue **R**omanus*); and they made good use of that epistolary formula **S.V.B.E.E.V.** (***S**i **v**ales, **b**ene **e**st, **e**go **v**aleo*)."

Huh? Say what??

Potter, the distinguished British linguist (1898–1976) from whom we last heard in Chapter 1, undoubtedly assumed he was addressing an erudite audience educated by stern taskmasters in tough English boarding schools. He never expected the day would come when every window washer was not conversant in Latin, and so he did not bother to supply English translations.

Let us explain. The first term, which precedes a

number, means "In the year from the founding of the city;" the Roman system of dating counts 753 B.C.E. as year 1. (The abbreviation is more often expanded as *Ab urbe condita.*) The second means "The senate and people of Rome." You may have seen the letters inscribed on standards lofted ceremoniously by extras in toga movies. And the third is "If you are well, it is well; I am well, too." This cordial notation foreshadows the romantic acronyms that became popular in World War II correspondence; see page 97.

In 63 B.C.E., Marcus Tullius Tiro, a freed slave who was secretary to the Roman orator Cicero, devised a system of abbreviations called the *notae Tironianae,* or Tironian notes. This shorthand technique was used to record the speeches of Roman senators. (An innovation of questionable merit!) Widely taught and practiced, the Tironian system lasted for more than a thousand years.

Tiro is said to have invented about five hundred abbreviations. Among them is the ampersand—which still is sometimes called "the Tironian sign." Tiro's version, however, looked more like a **7** than our modern **&**. This symbol was once placed at the *end* of the alphabet. Thus, when writing or reciting the alphabet, one would conclude: ". . . X, Y, Z, and *per se* [by itself] &." The phrase *and per se and* became ampersand. A reminder of the Latin *et* is still visible in the italic ampersand: *&*. Some enthusiastic writers centuries ago routinely used it even *within* words: for example, *h&some.*

Early Abbreviation Devices

Let us take a brief chronological digression to examine some pioneering forms of abbreviation.

Once phonetic language got rolling, abbreviations quickly proliferated. The Egyptians, Maccabean Jews, Christians, Greeks, and Romans all made good use of them. In the confined spaces of coins, the Romans inscribed **IMP CAES** for ***Imperator Caesar***. To conserve labor and space, similarly truncated inscriptions were chiseled into tombstones and temples.

Several techniques were common. Retaining the beginning of the word and dropping the rest was called *suspension*. With the omission of all but the first letter or letters, the one remaining character represented the complete word. For example, **F.** stood for *familia;* **ED.** for ***edictum***. This device is clearly the precursor of today's initialisms. In ancient Rome, single-letter abbreviations were called *sigla* (the plural of *siglum*) or *litterae singulares*.

Beginning in the fourth century of the current era, *contraction*, the omission of the middle letters, came into use. Examples: **scs** for ***sanctus,*** and **no.** (still in use) for ***numero.***

With both techniques, a punctuation mark often substitutes for the deleted element and signals that the term is a shortened form. One such device is a horizontal line called a *macron*, placed above the character or characters that remain. For example, **Ds** or **DS** stood for the Latin ***Deus***, God. Similarly,

$\overline{\mathbf{ss}}$ was the contracted form of *semis*, one half. Another device was a stroke or crossbar through a letter. Many other symbols originated as cursive flourishes in handwritten documents, later to be adopted in printed texts.

The period, which originated in the Roman, uh, period, ultimately replaced the macron, and remains a common abbreviation symbol today. (Our familiar apostrophe was invented much later, in the sixteenth century.)

A *ligature* does not delete letters but conserves space by squeezing them together, as in **æ** or **Æ.** You'll sometimes see the device in reproductions of old printed or handwritten documents. But the ligature is today little used, except in a few specialized disciplines such as musical notation, where, for example, ***ff*** represents *fortissimo*.

In Latin, plurals were sometimes indicated by *doubling* the abbreviation. This device is still used occasionally, as in **pp.** for **p**ages and **MSS.** for **m**anu**s**cript**s**.

The use of *superscripts* to indicate contraction and suspension, as in $\mathbf{4^{th}}$, also began in ancient times, and the technique lasted for centuries. In England and in colonial America, **Sam**uel was written as $\mathbf{Sam^{l}}$, and **servant** as $\mathbf{sev^{t}}$, to cite just two of hundreds of instances. The obsolescence of this practice may have been due to the introduction of the typewriter, which could not easily reproduce these "superior letters."

As you might expect, writers throughout history

devised their own abbreviations at will and whim. No official boards or language columnists decreed which were right and wrong. The consequences were predictable. Even in the ancient world, abbreviations proliferated to the point where they caused confusion. In the year 438 of the current era, the Roman Empire issued a prohibition on their use in legal documents; other bans followed under the Byzantine ruler Justinian I in 533 and 534.

Religious Iconography

Forward to the past.

The letters **IHS**, which appear on Christian ceremonial objects, are a contraction of ***Iesous,*** Greek for Jesus. The middle letter is not our Roman H but the capital form of the Greek letter *eta.* Since 1424, however, such misinterpretation has created the notion that the letters are an abbreviation for the Latin ***I****n* ***h****oc* ***s****igno* (In this sign) or ***I****esus* ***H****ominum* ***S****alvator* (Jesus, Savior of Man). Through the centuries, numerous other Latin and English expansions have been given to the letters.

Roman soldiers mockingly used the phrase ***I****esus* ***N****azarenus* ***R****ex* ***I****udaeorum,* or "Jesus of Nazareth, King of the Jews." By order of Pontius Pilate, the inscription **I.N.R.I.** was affixed to the cross. The letters often appear in artistic representations of the Crucifixion.

Since the second century, the image of a fish has been a universal symbol of Christ. The sign was used as a secret code or password among early Christians who suffered persecution under the Romans. To indicate their sympathies or designate a meeting place, believers could draw a simple outline, then quickly erase it.

The Greek word for fish is *ichthys,* and the letters **ICHTHYS** (pronounced "ICK-thoos") were construed as ***I**esous* ***Ch**ristos,* ***Th**eou* ***Y**ios,* ***S**oter* (Jesus Christ, God's Son, Savior). The choice of symbol was probably also intended to echo two familiar elements of Christian lore: the story of the loaves and fishes, and Jesus's appeal to fishermen to become "fishers of men." To this day, young evangelicals display the symbol on clothing and jewelry. It has been called the most famous Christian acronym.

If the spellings of Jesus in the preceding paragraphs appear puzzling, here's the explanation. The letter J is one of the most recent additions to the alphabet. No such letter existed in biblical times. Originally J was simply a variation of I. It became differentiated from that letter only in the mid-seventeenth century, and did not acquire a completely independent identity and function until the eighteenth. For all those millennia, J was read as either i or y. The sound we know and use today is from the influence of French.

The Middle Ages

In the medieval period, abbreviations became common. An estimated thirteen thousand were used. Writing materials were expensive, and the process of creating documents by hand was laborious and time-consuming. (No desktop publishing or photocopiers!) Understandably, monks who painstakingly inscribed manuscripts were motivated to borrow various calligraphic shortcuts from early Greek and Latin, and to devise their own.

The *Book of Kells,* the famous illuminated manuscript of the Gospels created in Scotland and Ireland in the eighth and ninth centuries, contains many abbreviations, such as **SPS** for ***Spiritus***, a contraction that, as you might have guessed, was adopted from Roman documents. As this example indicates, devices migrated among cultures, with some subsequently to reach our own.

Primitive peoples believe that language possesses magic powers and properties. Words and names have been viewed as keys to metaphysical secrets and supernatural knowledge. Seers and mystics tended to read acronyms into everything.

Cabala (sometimes transliterated as *kabbalah* and other spellings) is a system of Hebrew mysticism, developed between the seventh and twelfth centuries of the current era. Its practitioners perceived all sorts of symbolism and magic in arrangements of letters. A cabalistic art called *notarikon* interpreted a sentence by using selected letters to construct a new word.

These beliefs help us understand the motivation behind such reinterpretations as ICHTHYS. The term *notarikon,* by the way, derives from Greek, where it had a less mystical sense. It simply meant a shorthand writer, or abbreviation or shorthand *per se.*

During the Middle Ages, several prominent Jewish scholars had acronymic names. **Ra**bbi **Sh**lomo **Y**itzhaki (1040–1105) was called **Rashi**, and **Ra**bbi **M**oses **b**en **M**aimon (1135–1204) was **Rambam**, although today he is better remembered as Maimonides.

In 1494, what may have been the first dictionary of abbreviations, *Modus Legendi Abbreviaturas in utroque jure,* was published in Nuremberg. By 1613, abbreviations in Hebrew writings had become so widespread, ambiguous, and inconsistent (a problem often noted today!) that Christians, eager to study these texts, couldn't make head or tail of them. So Johannes Buxtorf the Elder, a distinguished Christian scholar of Hebrew literature, compiled *De Abbreviaturis Hebraicis.* Many other glossaries of abbreviations were to follow (see Appendix II).

In their experiments, sixteenth-century alchemists used **vitriol**. It was not scathing invective, a later metaphor, but sulfuric acid or any of the several metallic sulfates. The word was mystically reinterpreted by those early scientists to mean ***V**isita **I**nteriora **T**errae **R**ectificando **I**nvenies **O**ccultum **L**apidem,* or "Visit the interior of the earth and by right action you will find the occult stone."

Francis Bacon (1561–1626) is the English philosopher and politician sometimes credited with writing Shakespeare's plays. As a child, he supposedly heard the prophecy "When Hempe is spun, England's done." **HEMPE**, the story goes, stood for the rulers of England: **H**enry, **E**dward, **M**ary and **P**hilip, **E**lizabeth. As is often the case with cryptic forecasts, however, the chaos that many expected did not occur, but the prophecy nevertheless "came true." According to *Brewer's Dictionary of Phrase and Fable:* "At the close of the last reign [1603, when Elizabeth died] 'England was done,' since the sovereign [James, her successor] no longer styled himself 'King of England' but 'King of Great Britain and Ireland.' "

The Renaissance

Throughout history, members of royalty, the nobility, and the church have adopted slogans in acronymic and initialistic form. These devices were incorporated into the designs of family crests and coats of arms.

As early as the fifteenth century, various Austrian emperors used the letters **A.E.I.O.U.** for this purpose. (Vanna White would undoubtedly approve.) As one leader replaced another, each gave the letters different expansions, first in Latin, then in German. One English version: "**A**ustria's **E**mpire **I**s **O**verall **U**niversal." After the War of 1866, however, irreverent wits suggested "**A**ustria's **E**mpire **I**s **O**usted **U**tterly."

The motto of Elisabeth Ernestine Antonie, Duchess of Saxony (1681–1766), was **TANDEM**, or *Tibi **A**derit **N**umen **D**ivinum, **E**xpecta **M**odo* (God will help thee; only wait). The acronym is especially apt because *tandem* is Latin for "at length" or "finally."

The pseudonym of the English philosopher John Locke (1632–1704), whose political ideas influenced America's Founding Fathers, was **TARPTOLA**, for ***T**heologiae **A**pud **R**emonstrantes **P**rofessorem, **T**yrannidis **O**sorem, **L**imburgium **A**mstelodamensem.* It translates as "Theology Professor Among the Remonstrants, Hater of Tyranny, the Limburgian of Amsterdam." Locke lived in the Netherlands for five years because he was suspected of conspiring in a plot against the British government. The Remonstrants were adherents of one side of a complex religious dispute.

An anti-Episcopal tract that appeared in 1641, in response to a book by Bishop Hall of Norwich, was titled **SMECTYMNUUS**, for the initials of its creators: **S**teven **M**arshall, **E**dward **C**alamy, **T**homas **Y**oung, **M**atthew **N**ewcomen, and **W**illiam (W = double U) **S**purstow. The pseudonymous title was probably chosen in an effort to conceal the identities of the authors. (Just in case you ever need to know, it's pronounced "smeck-TIM-nyoo-us.") This technique is still occasionally used for scientific papers written by teams. For example, five scientists who collaborated on a study of the possible effects of nuclear war (R. P. **T**urco, O. B. **T**oon, T. P. **A**ckerman, J. B. **P**ollack, and Carl **S**agan) are referred to as **TTAPS**.

Linguistic condensation continued apace. In the late seventeenth and early eighteenth centuries, notes Joseph Shipley, "it became fashionable to speak in fragments of words, much as now we speak of new projects by their initials."

Some of these once-popular abbreviations are now extinct, such as *ult* for *ultimate* and *pozz* for *positively*. Others remain in use today. One example is *mob,* a clipping of the Latin *mobile vulgus,* Latin for "excitable crowd."

Even back then, the critics were up in arms. The English satirist Jonathan Swift (1667–1745), author of *Gulliver's Travels,* condemned "that barbarous custom of abbreviating words" into harsh monosyllables and "manglings." This abuse, he charged, spoils the language. Besides the clippings cited above, he disliked contractions and elisions that omitted the "e" in the past tense of verbs, such as *disturb'd.*

Despite his professed distaste for the practice, Swift employed affectionate initialisms (such as **Ppt** for **p**oor **p**retty **t**hing) in his famous journal of love letters to "Stella" (Esther Johnson), written between 1710 and 1713.

Swift's contemporary Joseph Addison (1672–1719), the English poet and essayist, also complained about the abbreviating habit "which has so miserably curtailed some of our words." Like Swift, Addison's animus toward abbreviation seems curious if not disingenuous. Addison's pseudonym was Clio. Although Clio is the muse of history, the name had an additional meaning. Addison signed each of his articles in *The Spectator* with one of the letters **C**, **L**, **I**, **O**. They represented the venues where he wrote: **C**helsea, **L**ondon, **I**slington, and "The **O**ffice."

During the reign of William III (1689–1702), the curious expression **Limp** was a Jacobite toast. No sexual pejorative implied! It was an acronym created from the initials of **L**ouis XIV, **J**ames II, **M**ary of Modena (James's daughter and William's wife), and the **P**rince of Wales. (The letters J and I were then used interchangeably.)

Nineteenth-century America

Time marched on. The centuries turned. Like many immigrants seeking their fortune in the New World, abbreviations and acronyms journeyed to America.

"Beginning in the summer of 1838," wrote Allen Walker Read in *American Speech*, "there developed in Boston a remarkable vogue of using abbreviations. It might well be called a craze."

Newspapers casually studded their pages with silly initialisms, most apparently invented for the occasion, helpfully "translating" them for the reader. A few samples: **O.F.M.** (**o**ur **f**irst **m**en), **R.T.B.S.** (**r**emains **t**o **b**e **s**een), **G.T.D.H.D.** (**g**ive **t**he **d**evil **h**is **d**ue), and **T.B.F.T.B.** (**t**oo **b**ig **f**or **t**heir **b**ritches).

During the 1830s, many Americans indulged in a passion for puns, facetious misspellings, jocular neologisms, and other language play. Fraternal groups and societies boasted lengthy names that were routinely abbreviated; imbibers ordered mixed drinks by their initials; and conversations were peppered with slang such as **S.P.** (**s**mall **p**otatoes).

By 1839, the initialism fad had spread from Boston to New York and New Orleans. Abbreviations also flourished way out West circa 1835, where they were, according to one view, independently pioneered.

Although the wordplay was humorously intended, some proper citizens were puzzled and annoyed. Like critics before and since, they voiced their denunciations in angry letters to newspaper editors. But to no avail. At least one coinage from this period endured: **O.K.**, about which more on page 111.

The Twentieth Century

The purposes acronyms serve are not always innocent. Mystery writer Donald E. Westlake recounts that about 1900, New York merchants seeking employees posted signs in their windows. The words "Help Wanted" were often followed by **NINA**. No, the shop owner wasn't looking for a clerk by that name. The coded euphemism meant "**N**o **I**rish **n**eed **a**pply."

The force that landed at Gallipoli in 1915 was called **ANZAC**, for **A**ustralian and **N**ew **Z**ealand **A**rmy **C**orps. The coinage is attributed to Lieutenant General Sir W. R. Birdwood, commander of the corps. Australian and New Zealand soldiers thus came to be called **ANZAC**s. To this day, the term resonates patriotically down under.

About 1923, C. K. Ogden of Cambridge University began devising his system of "**Basic** English." An acronym of the words **B**ritish, **A**merican, **S**cientific, **I**nternational, and **C**ommercial, the simplified system of 850 words was intended to help foreigners learn English and to make communication more efficient. Despite endorsements from Franklin Delano Roosevelt and Winston Churchill, it failed to catch on.

The New Deal era (1933–39) brought the much-derided "alphabet agencies": **W.P.A.** (**W**orks **P**rogress **A**dministration), **C.C.C.** (**C**ivilian **C**onservation **C**orps), **O.P.A.** (**O**ffice of **P**rice **A**dministration), and many more, some still with us. A few patriotic parents named their baby girls **Nira**, after the 1933 **N**ational **I**ndustrial **R**ecovery **A**ct, the legislation that created the less euphonious **N.R.A.**, for National Recovery Administration. Perhaps it's more than coincidental that **F.D.R.** was the first President to be widely known by his initials.

New York governor Al Smith is credited with coining the disparaging locution "alphabet soup." It still aptly characterizes Washington officialese, though perhaps "pea soup" would be a more appropriate appetizer for the inhabitants of Foggy Bottom.

During World War II, the proliferation of initialisms and acronyms accelerated.

In his 1988 memoir *Washington Goes to War,* David Brinkley recalls: "Six months into the war, there were so many new agencies, all known by their initials, nobody could keep them straight. . . . One office, issuing wartime regulations for plumbers, was the PWPGSJSISIACWPB."

Other acronymic coinages from the war era include **SHAPE**, **S**upreme **H**eadquarters, **A**llied **P**owers, **E**urope; and **ASDIC**, from **A**nti-**S**ubmarine **D**etection **I**nvestigation **C**ommittee. **ASDIC** was a type of sonar invented in Britain in 1939. (For more about **sonar**, itself an acronym, see the next chapter.)

The **p**ipe **l**ine **u**nder **t**he **o**cean, or **PLUTO**, was a 1945 British scheme to transport gasoline under the English Channel to Allied forces on the Continent. Pluto, the god of the underworld, was an apt name.

V.I.P. originated in Army usage during World War II. It was often used derisively, for someone who only *thinks* he's important. During that period, a **v**ery **i**mportant **p**erson was also termed a "viper." This version proved to be short-lived—and no wonder!

The two world wars also sparked a resurgence of the fad, which we earlier noted had its origins in ancient Rome, of inscribing cryptic acronyms on envelope flaps.

SWAK (**S**ealed **w**ith **a** **k**iss) is still with us. But lovers separated by continents followed that message with **BOLTOP** (**B**etter **o**n **l**ips **t**han **o**n **p**aper). Also popular were the geographically seductive **MALAYA** (**M**y **a**nxious **l**ips **a**wait **y**our **a**rrival), **POLAND** (**P**lease **o**pen **l**ovingly **a**nd **n**ever **d**estroy), **ITALY** (**I** **t**rust **a**nd **l**ove **y**ou), and **HOLLAND** (**H**ope [or **H**ere] **o**ur **l**ove **l**ives [or **l**asts] **a**nd **n**ever **d**ies). Some were more provocative: **BURMA** (**B**e **u**ndressed, **r**eady, **m**y **a**ngel) and the liberally spelled **NORWICH** (**K**n**ickers** **o**ff; **r**eady **w**hen **I** **c**ome **h**ome).

Although the coded messages undoubtedly pleased and amused the romantic couples, one wonders what wartime censors made of them. Did they assume the writers (mostly British servicemen) were informing the enemy of planned invasion sites?

One event we bypassed is the development of shorthand and stenography (also called *brachygraphy,* short writing, and *tachygraphy,* swift writing) since the time of Tiro. Between the sixteenth and nineteenth centuries, ingenious British inventors developed numerous rapid-writing methods. The eponymous systems of Pitman and Gregg are still used. Equally industrious Germans and Americans tinkered with speedwriting methods well into the twentieth century. For English alone, an estimated four hundred or more of these systems were created.

Yet no shorthand devices seem to have become everyday English abbreviations. Why not? David Crystal, in *The Cambridge Encyclopedia of Language,* explains that because such systems are intended for a limited audience, and relatively ephemeral purposes, they are prone to idiosyncratic use. "It is quite common," Crystal observes, "for secretaries trained in the same system to be unable to read each other's shorthand."

So ends our history of abbreviation, bringing us to the present. Other historical items may be found in the sections on military usage (Chapter 6, page 172) and foreign language acronyms (Chapter 7). The surprisingly recent creation of the word *acronym* was discussed in Chapter 1, page 27.

In the next chapter we shall return to various periods and places as we survey coinages that have become standard English words, and some words whose purported acronymic origins are apocryphal.

CHAPTER 4

❖

Remarkable Etymologies: Words All Readers Doubtlessly Savor (REWARDS)

How does an acronym enter popular usage, gain acceptance, and—sometimes—become a "real" word, part of our language?

Any new word or new meaning for an existing word is called a *neologism.* If the word is created by design, as opposed to gradual evolution from previous forms, it is a *coinage.*

A neologism may well prove ephemeral, a fad. A word coined and used for a specific occasion is a *nonce word.* If it is created primarily for effect, to display cleverness, lexicographers call it a *stunt word.* But sometimes a coinage survives and enters the English language. Although the results may not always be ideal, they help to expand the boundaries of language.

Certain words we use every day were born as acronyms. Others are popularly *assumed* to be acronyms but in reality are *not.* In this chapter we examine specimens from both categories, real and mythical, and the stories behind them.

The familiar words in the next two sections were all originally acronyms. Having entered the language, most are now fully *lower-cased*—that is, neither all caps nor initial-capped. They are presented in a sequence that logically groups terms by their meanings, rather than in alphabetical or chronological order. The parenthetical dates indicate when the word was coined, or first recorded, according to (in most cases) *The Oxford English Dictionary,* which is regarded as the definitive historical reference work on the language.

Scientific and Technical Acronym Words

We have noted that progress generates the need for new names. So it's not surprising that so many acronymic words are terms from science and technology.

radar (1935), as every driver should know, was coined from **ra**dio **d**etection **a**nd **r**anging. Although invented in England in 1935 and used by the Allies throughout World War II for aerial navigation and the detection of enemy planes (assisting in the defeat of Germany in the Battle of Britain in 1940), radar only became known to the public in 1941. Until then, the technology, and even the word, were closely guarded military secrets.

sonar (1945), a system for detecting objects underwater, is from **so**und **na**vigation **r**anging. (The **a** is sometimes construed as representing **a**nd.) In the previous chapter, we briefly mentioned ASDIC, another device with the same purpose.

loran (1942), **lo**ng-**ra**nge **n**avigation, helps a ship identify its position by calculating the difference in the arrival times of signals from two transmitting stations.

laser (1960), no longer science fiction but a ubiquitous component of C.D. players and supermarket checkout scanners, means **l**ight **a**mplification by **s**timulated **e**mission of **r**adiation. A laser is also called an "optical maser," **maser** (1955) being **m**icrowave **a**mplification by **s**timulated **e**mission of **r**adiation.

Taser (1972) is a nonlethal stun gun that fires electrified barbs. Thc inventor coined the word, on the model of laser, by juggling the letters of the imaginary (and imaginative) **T**om **S**wift **a**nd his **e**lectric **r**ifle. (Sometimes it's the more elegant expansion **T**homas **A. S**wift's **e**lectric **r**ifle.) The name is a trademark.

Bren gun, or simply **Bren** (1937), is a British light automatic weapon, from **Br**no, Czechoslovakia, where it was developed, and **En**field, England, where it was manufactured.

bev (about 1945) is a unit of energy measuring 1 **b**illion **e**lectron **v**olts. A nuclear accelerator called a bevatron produces energy in multiples of those extremely high units.

rem (1947) is **r**oentgen **e**quivalent in **m**an, the amount of ionizing radiation that produces an effect in an organism equal to one roentgen of X rays. Because it measures medical damage, the unit is useful in establishing safe limits for radiation exposure. Among other places, such radiation would be released in a nuclear explosion. (In 1957, **REM** also became **r**apid **e**ye **m**ovement, a stage of sleep.)

The following two examples are syllabic acronyms:

cyborg (1960) is a **cyb**ernetic **org**anism. Neuroscientist Manfred Clynes coined the word, a science-fictional fusing of man and machine that is endowed with superhuman capabilities. It's a predecessor of *bionic.*

parsec (1913), **par**allax **sec**ond, is the distance light travels in 3.26 years, a unit of distance in interstellar space. (A Boeing project is called **PARSECS**, **P**rogram for **A**stronomical **R**esearch and **S**cientific **E**xperiments **C**oncerning **S**pace.)

The next two scientific terms are not acronyms but *blends,* taking the first and *final* syllables of other words. Nevertheless, we are including them to make a point or two.

quasar (1964) is from **quasi**-stell**ar** radio source, a celestial object that emits powerful radio waves and is located approximately 4 billion to 10 billion light-years away. (Don't forget your American Express card!)

pulsar (1968) is a **pul**sating st**ar.** If this phenomenon turns out to be caused by intelligent beings, it can be redefined, some suggest, as **p**ulsed **u**niform **l**aser-**s**timulated **a**rtificial **r**adiation. Note that this latter expansion represents a *true* acronym, and one that incorporates *another* acronym. (About 1970, the first digital L.E.D. watch carried the trade name Pulsar; the name is still used by Seiko for some of its quartz watches.)

More Genuine Acro-words

Nontechnical language can also be acronymic. Consider the following examples:

Diving equipment requiring no cumbersome paraphernalia that umbilically connects the explorer to the surface is called **scuba** (1952), which is from **s**elf-**c**ontained **u**nderwater **b**reathing **a**pparatus.

A **quango** (1967) is a **qua**si **n**on**go**vernmental **o**rganization. Sometimes the expansion is given as

quasi-**a**utonomous. Whatever, it's not an exotic tropical bird but a semipublic agency that performs governmental functions, akin to our U.S.P.S. since it was privatized (sort of) by Congress. Strangely enough, although quangos are mostly found in the U.K., the term appears to have originated in the good old U.S.A.

One acronymic word is universally known: **snafu**, which originated in World War II, about 1940. In its slightly bowdlerized version, the word derives from the phrase **s**ituation **n**ormal: **a**ll **f**ouled **up**.

"It offered a satirical summary of all that most of us objected to in military life—red tape, indecision, confusion over which no one seemed to have any control," wrote Lieutenant Jeffery A. Fleece in a 1946 issue of *American Speech.*

The word entered dictionaries and inspired many variations, but none has acquired the widespread currency of the original parent coinage. Among the spin-offs (here rendered in all caps to signify their nonstandard status): **FUBAR** (**f**ouled **u**p **b**eyond **a**ll **r**ecognition), **SAPFU** (**s**urpassing **a**ll **p**revious **f**oul-**u**ps), **CUMMFU** (**c**omplete **u**tter **m**onumental **m**ilitary **f**oul-**up**), and **JANFU** (**j**oint **A**rmy-**N**avy **f**oul-**up**). Who says the armed forces can't cooperate? Service personnel have created numerous other **fu**'s, with a prolixity limited only by their imaginations.

Wasps, Yuppies, and Others

A **Wasp** or **WASP** is, of course, a **W**hite **A**nglo-**S**axon **P**rotestant, carrying the implicit connotation of old wealth.

The date of origin for Wasp has been cited everywhere between 1960 and 1964, but Andrew Hacker used it in the sociological life-style sense in a speech he delivered, and published, in 1957. Some criticize the term as redundant (*all* Anglo-Saxons are white); others insist that it's disparaging. Indeed, according to one theory, Wasp was coined as a deliberate rebuke of slurs directed against ethnic minorities. It carries, notes Irving Allen in *Maledicta,* the implications of bourgeois conformity and spiritual emptiness. And *waspish* means snappish and spiteful. (In Israel, a Wasp is a "**W**hite **A**shkenazi **S**abra with **P**ull.")

Everyone knows that a **y**oung **u**rban (or **u**pwardly mobile) **p**rofessional is a **yuppie**—or **yuppy**. The three-letter acronymic base quickly acquired a *hypocoristic suffix*—a diminutive ending analogous to those in pet names and nicknames, such as Johnnie or Johnny for John. The formation is modeled on and echoes **yippie**, itself a 1968 acronym from **Y**outh **I**nternational **P**arty, and *hippie,* which dates back to the 1950s. (During World War II, a **yippie** was a Navy harbor boat, a pseudo-acronym from **Y.P.**, the initialism for **y**ard **p**atrol.)

Bob Greene, the *Chicago Tribune* syndicated columnist, reported that he overheard "yuppie" in a bar, and he is generally credited with using the word in print for the first time. That historic date: March 23, 1983. Despite claims to the contrary, Greene denies coining the word. Although sometimes used favorably, it was apparently intended from the outset as disparaging. *The Yuppie Handbook* (1984), by Marissa Piesman and Marilee Hartley, helped give the word currency, and the trend was under way.

By one count, no fewer than eighty "life-style classifications" or "sociological acronyms" exist, of which we shall here examine only a sampling. Demographers, marketers, and market researchers use them to divide the population into segments.

Some of these appellations are used seriously, while others are facetious. Sometimes, however, it's hard to tell the difference! Although they are often lower-cased, we elect to place all but yuppie in all capital letters, as most have not qualified as "real" words—so far. Many are clearly ephemeral nonce forms or stunt words.

A **y**oung **u**pwardly **m**obile **p**rofessional is more accurately a **YUMPIE**. Ergo, a **GRUMP** or **GRUMPIE** is a **g**rim, **r**uthless, **u**pwardly **m**obile **p**rofessional. A **BUPPIE** or **BUMPIE** is a **b**lack **ur**ban (**u**pwardly **m**obile) **p**rofessional. A **FUPPIE** is a **f**emale **u**rban **p**rofessional. A **PUPPIE** is a **p**regnant **u**rban **p**rofessional. A **MUPPIE** is a **m**iddle-aged **ur**ban **p**rofessional. A **YUMMY** is a **y**oung **u**pwardly **m**obile **m**other—a term coined by the magazine *Redbook* to define its readers to advertisers. (The spelling of the suffix was undoubtedly chosen to parallel *mommy* and *mummy.*)

In *After Six Days,* a novel by Keith Harrison, a Canadian yuppie is a **YAWNIE,** a **y**oungish **A**nglophone of **W**estmount and **N**otre-Dame-de-Grâce (two upscale Montreal neighborhoods). A clever coinage, but it never caught on.

As the 1980s drew to a close, the U.S. economy went into a tailspin. Some yuppies turned into **YUFFIE**s (**y**oung **u**rban **f**ailures) or **DUMPIE**s (**d**ownwardly **m**obile **p**rofessionals), an evocative if imperfect coinage. Meanwhile, the **SCUPPIE** (**so**cially **c**onscious **u**rban **p**rofessional) is a poor but activist type who presumably exemplifies the kinder and gentler 1990s.

Breaking the rhythmic pattern, a **DOMO** is a **do**wnwardly **mo**bile professional who voluntarily abandons a successful but frustrating job for a more fulfilling alternative career, while a **SWELL** is a **s**ingle **w**oman **e**arning **l**ots and **l**ots, and a **MOSS** is a **m**iddle-aged, **o**verstressed, **s**emi-affluent **s**uburbanite.

Other age groups, both less and more mature, have not been ignored. **PUP**, **p**re-**u**rban **p**rofessional, was coined by *Teenage* magazine. A **f**un-**l**oving **y**outh **e**n **r**oute to success is a **FLYER:** a thirteen- to twenty-five-year-old who is hipper, we are reliably informed, than a yuppie. **SKIPPIE**s or **SKIPPER**s are **s**ociety's **k**ids **i**n their **p**arents' **p**ockets—or **s**chool **k**ids with **i**ncome and **p**urchasing **p**ower. Their grandmother or grandfather might be a **WOOP** or **WOOPIE**, **w**ell-**o**ff **o**lder **p**erson; an **OPAL**, **o**lder **p**erson with **a**ctive **l**ife-style; a **RASP**, **r**emarkable **a**ging **s**mart **p**erson; or a **WORM**, **w**hite **o**lder **r**ich **m**an.

A frequently cited demographic acronym is **DINK**. This term refers to a hardworking couple possessing **d**ouble **i**ncome, **n**o **k**ids. The variant **DINKY** appends ". . . **y**et," which is not only ambiguous in meaning (do they or don't they have parental aspirations?) but also could be construed as an adjective with a different meaning. (The **D** is sometimes rendered as **d**ual.)

This construction inspired **MINK**, **m**ultiple **in**come, **n**o **k**ids; **TICK**, **t**wo-**i**ncome **c**ouple with **k**ids; and **OINK**, **o**ne **i**ncome, **n**o **k**id. (Sometimes the **o** means zero, which is quite different!) A 1987 *Time* article suggested two presumably jocular variations: **NINK**, **n**o **i**ncome, **n**o **k**ids; and **TIPS**, **t**iny **i**ncome, **p**arents **s**upporting.

Single **i**ncome, **t**wo **c**hildren, **o**utrageous **mo**rtgage spells **SITCOM,** a contrived and possibly facetious coinage. (In the television industry sense, sitcom is a syllabic acronym or blend.)

An earlier version of the yuppie that didn't make the journey into popular parlance is **YAVIS** (**y**oung, **a**ttractive [sometimes **a**daptable], **v**erbal, **i**ntelligent, **s**uccessful). The term was used by therapists to describe desirable patients: those who could benefit most from treatment, or perhaps were able to afford the fees.

POSSLQ (pronounced "possel-cue") means **p**erson(s) of **o**pposite **s**ex **s**haring **l**iving **q**uarters. The Census Bureau, seeking a nonjudgmental and politically correct term to describe the inhabitants of a household, coined it for the 1980 census. (That the census people are fond of acronyms is indicated by their **T**opical **I**ntegrated **G**eographic **E**ncoding and **R**eferencing system, or **TIGER**.)

Inspired by the neologism, CBS commentator Charles Osgood wrote a funny poem on the subject, a line of which gave him the memorable title of his 1981 book: *There's Nothing That I Wouldn't Do If You Would Be My POSSLQ.*

Incidentally, how *do* you introduce a roommate to whom you are not married? To solve this knotty dilemma, many ideas have been suggested; the most elegant is *covivant.*

Macho men who have reformed are **SNAG**s: **s**ensitive **n**ew **a**ge **g**uys. But note well: The term is usually employed derisively by skeptical females who think it's all an act! Other humorous coinages include **BURPIES** (**b**oozing **u**rban-**r**ural **p**arasites) and **CHUMP** (**ch**ild of **u**pwardly **m**obile **p**rofessionals).

Ethnics include **JUPPIE** (Japanese), **CHUPPIE** (Chinese), and **HUPPIE** (Hispanic). A **YUCA** or **YUCCA** is a **y**oung, **u**p-and-**c**oming **C**uban-**A**merican; it's also a pun on the Spanish word for cassava. A **GUPPIE** is a **g**ay **u**rban **p**rofessional. A **YUMMIE** or **YUMMY** has been defined here and in the United Kingdom as referring to, variously: . . . **M**uslim,

Marxist, or **m**inister, in addition to the **m**oms noted earlier.

Speaking of Britain, we like some of the coinages over there:

GLAMs are forty-five- to fifty-nine-year-olds who are **g**raying, **l**eisured, **a**ffluent, **m**arried (or **m**iddle-aged). A suddenly wealthy individual, usually over forty, is a **PIPPIE**: **p**erson **i**nheriting **p**arents' **p**roperty.

But the ultimate appellation may be **LOMBARD**, meaning **l**ots **o**f **m**oney **b**ut **a** **r**eal **d**ickhead. (Variant expansions substitute **l**oads and **r**ight.) Interestingly enough, Lombard is an old name for a banker or moneylender, and Lombard Street is a London financial center. The coinage is outstanding, but British friends tell me it's not in common use. Too bad.

"Initialism Words"

Sometimes a new word is created by sounding out phonetically the individual letters of what is at first an initialism.

Not clear? A few illustrations will explain it all for you.

The broadcasting term **emcee** derives from **M.C.**, for **m**aster of **c**eremonies. Equally familiar is **deejay**, from **D.J.**, short for **d**isc **j**ockey, and the more recent **veejay** for **V.J.**, for **v**ideo **j**ockey. Similarly, **Jaycees** belong to the **J**unior **C**hamber of

Commerce, while **Jayvees** are **j**unior **v**arsity members.

The **seabee** is from **C.B.** (**C**onstruction **B**atallion, formed in 1942 as **N.C.B.**, the **N** for **N**aval). Appropriately, the name evokes the image of a hive of busy nautical insects. (In the British military, however, **C.B.** means **c**onfined to **b**arracks.)

The most popular example of this species? It's **O.K.** with us!

Because the initials sound like **okay**, the expression evolved into that variant spelling. It is simultaneously an initialism and a word, and both forms remain in common use. It is employed as a noun, a verb, an adverb, an adjective, and an interjection. Note, however, that O.K. is *not* an acronym; if it were, it would be pronounced *oak*. (It sometimes *is*, as in *okey-doke* and other annoying variations, but that's another story—or book.)

O.K. is "unquestionably the single most universally used and useful of human utterances," observes Gary Jennings in *World of Words*.

Yet it probably has more suggested etymologies, both serious and fanciful, than any other English word. According to various accounts, O.K. supposedly dervives from Choctaw *okeh* ("it is so"), Louisiana French *au quai* ("to the wharf," a mark designating bales of cotton approved for shipping), Haitian French (a rum named *Aux Cayes*), and Mandingo or Wolof or Ewe, African languages where it (or a variation) means "good" or "all right," by way of black American slang.

Yet another story credits the coinage to Andrew Jackson, who supposedly misspelled **O.R.**, meaning **o**rder **r**ecorded, in a 1790 court document; to a telegrapher's abbreviation of **o**pen **k**ey; to the Indian chief **O**ld **K**eokuk; to biscuits sold by **O**rrin **K**endall; to **O.K.** sauce . . . and the list goes on.

In 1963 and 1964, in a series of articles in the journal *American Speech,* Columbia University Professor Allen Walker Read devoted to O.K. a more detailed analysis (108 pages and 540 footnotes!) than has perhaps been expended upon any other two-letter expression. The results of his exhaustive scholarship are generally regarded as definitive.

According to Professor Read, the locution originated in Boston in 1839. As we noted in Chapter 3, the city was then caught up in a fad for abbreviations and fanciful spellings, such as **O.W.** for **o**ll **w**right. On March 23, Bostonians awoke to read in their copies of the *Morning Post* the letters **O.K.** as an abbreviation of **o**ll **k**orrect, a deliberate misspelling of *all correct.*

The following year, the initialism became the slogan of the Democratic Party "O.K. Club." The politicos' choice was reinforced by the coincidence that the nickname of presidential candidate Martin Van Buren was "**O**ld **K**inderhook," after Kinderhook, his New York State hometown. Because of that campaign, O.K. "went national," and the rest is history.

Over the years, various writers have advanced other theories for the provenance of the expression (some people seem especially eager to establish an earlier date than Read's), and spurious explanations were rampant for decades. H. L. Mencken reproduced many of the mythical accounts and may have thus inadvertently perpetuated them. Read's articles, however, convincingly debunk all rival accounts.

A boxer who receives a **k**nock**o**ut or **K.O.** might be described as the *opposite* of O.K. In the pugilistic sense dating perhaps from 1914, K.O., later **kayo**, parallels the evolution of O.K. to okay: from an initialism to an "initialism word" to a word in its own right. (The two expressions, though etymologically unrelated, are irresistible targets for punsters.)

In the process of forming these initialism words, the abbreviation is, at least in written form, *expanded.* Some observers regard this development as a regression, or at least contradictory or ironic. But it's simply evidence of the human tendency to coin new words, a need that coexists with the urge to shorten them.

A related but slightly different form occurs when pronunciation and spelling conflate two letters to create a new word.

Like O.K., the origin of **Jeep** is enmeshed in numerous conflicting stories. Designed for the U.S. Army in 1940, the name was registered as a trademark the same year. (Several accounts assert earlier dates for both the invention and the naming of the versatile vehicle.)

Most explanations cite the term **G.P.** from **G**eneral **P**urpose vehicle, with the two letters phonetically coalescing into a single new word. Another interpretation holds that the car was named for "Eugene the Jeep," a tiny animal in the "Popeye" comic strip since 1936, who had uncanny powers to "do anything" (as the manufacturer and owners might well have believed of the vehicle), and who uttered the exclamation "jeep!" Finally, some assert that the name was influenced by *both* factors. (By the way, **JEEP** is also the **J**oint **E**mergency **E**vacuation **P**lan, which would spirit high-level Washington officials to safety in the event of a nuclear war.)

Similarly structured is **veep,** from **V.P.**, for **v**ice **p**resident. As with Jeep, a speaker or speller inserted the "ee" (or interpreted the first letter as "vee") to make the initialism into a pronounceable word. First used in 1949, veep referred to then Vice President Alben W. Barkley. In 1953, one Richard M. Nixon opined that the term was an affectionate tribute to his predecessor and should never be applied to anyone else. Despite that high-level recommendation, it's still used occasionally.

These specimens are not acronyms. This creature is an intriguing hybrid that occupies a middle ground in the bestiary of abbreviations. Perhaps it falls into the "pseudo-acronym" class we described earlier. It might alternatively be categorized as a variant of the "initialism word."

Finally, the prepossessing word **abecedarian** (1603) is an acronym or initialism word of sorts. It means a person learning the alphabet, or a beginner of any kind. As an adjective, it means "pertaining to the alphabet" (we used it in Chapter 3 to describe acrostics in the Bible), or to matters elementary. As you might guess, it was coined (originally in Latin as *abecedarium*) from the sounds of the Roman letters **A B C D**.

Mythical Acronyms: Apocryphal Awry

"Contrary to popular belief . . ."

Some words are frequently described as having been coined from acronyms, but almost certainly were *not*.

The apocryphal acronymic origins of these specimens are instances of *folk etymology,* the term for an incorrect but popularly believed story of a word's origin. (Some scholars prefer the term *spook etymology* for the examples that follow.) In reality, such words have more conventional and less glamorous beginnings. The purported acronym was coined afterward, by someone who cleverly matched a phrase to the letters. But despite the speciousness of the explanations, people believed them, and the tales gained currency.

Let us examine the alleged roots of these words, along with their more likely origins. The process may prove both enlightening and fun.

We begin with the often-heard yarn that **posh** (1918, perhaps earlier), meaning elegant or luxurious, is an acronym from the phrase "**p**ort **o**utward; **s**tarboard **h**ome." When wealthy folk cruised via steamer between Britain and India during the nineteenth century, these were supposedly the most desirable cabin locations, because the temperature was lower on the northeast side of the ship, away from the sun. The high-status initials, we are told, were stamped on the tickets.

Pretty colorful, no? But wrong. The true origin of posh is not known with certainty. Among various theories is that it is a truncation of *polished,* a slang word for *dandy,* or a colloquialism for money, from a halfpenny coin, which in turn comes from the Romany *påšh,* meaning half. Despite having been repeatedly debunked, some dictionaries and books of word origins still report as fact this entertaining acronymic legend.

The noun and verb **tip**, in the sense of gratuity (early eighteenth century), supposedly derives from the phrase **t**o **i**nsure **p**romptness. As the story goes, British travelers visiting inns and taverns handed cash to the waiter, along with a slip of paper inscribed with these three enticing letters. In another version, a box in London coffeehouses was conspicuously labeled **T.I.P.** But here's a hot tip: Don't buy it! As with posh, the real etymology cannot be confirmed, but one speculation is that it comes from "rogue's cant," where tip meant "to give"—originally anything, then money specifically. Or you might prefer the view that it's a clipping of s**tip**end.

The New England codfish known as **scrod** (1841) has been "explained" as an acronym meaning **s**pecial **c**atch **r**eceived **o**n **d**ock—allegedly a phrase inscribed on signs touting the day's haul, whatever it might be. Although it cannot be documented, the name may come from the Middle Dutch *schroode,* a verb meaning to strip or shred. (You won't catch us repeating the old joke about the visitor to Boston who asks everyone where he can get scrod.)

The colloquial **cop** (1859), for a police officer, supposedly comes from **c**onstable **o**n **p**atrol. Our response: Knock it off, or I'll run yez in! Another popular but equally suspect explanation is that it is a clipping of *copper* (also slang for policeman), which in turn is said to derive from the copper badges or buttons on police uniforms. The most authoritative sources say that cop is from the Latin *capere,* to take or capture.

While on the subject of crime, the verb **rob** does *not* stand for **r**elieve **o**f **b**ooty. It probably originated from the Old French *rober* in the early thirteenth century or before.

Equally fanciful is the story that **mafia** (early nineteenth century) comes from an ancient Sicilian slogan *"**M**orte **a**i **F**rancesi gl'**I**taliani **a**nelano"* ("Death to the French is the Italians' Cry"). Just the facts, ma'am! In Sicilian dialect, *mafia* originally meant courage, boldness, bravado. According to some sources, that word derives from the Arabic *mahyah,* meaning either boasting or "place of refuge." But an authoritative work on Italian etymologies disputes that cross-cultural explanation. The word may have acquired its acronymic redefinition in the 1860s, when the Italians were again opposing French invaders.

Another delightful but apocryphal tale concerns the word **news**. According to this account, the source is the four compass points: **n**orth, **e**ast, **w**est, **s**outh. *Extra! Read all about it!* In its modern sense, news goes way back to the early 1400s (but "in common use only after 1500," says the *Oxford English Dictionary*). It derives from the French *nouvelles*.

Some people wonder how the **vamp** (1911) of the silent screen could have evolved from the fireman who belonged to the **V**oluntary **A**ssociation of **M**aster **P**umpers. Well, she didn't. Vamps did indeed battle blazes in America in the 1870s. But in the sense of a scheming and seductive woman, vamp is a clipping of *vampire*.

Still more intriguing (pun intended) is the notion that **cabal** is an acronym constructed from the names of a group of ministers serving in the court of Charles II as his Privy Council foreign committee (1667–73). In 1672, the group secretly signed a treaty with France without the approval of Parliament, thus plunging England into a war with Holland. The five suspects: **C**lifford, **A**shley, **B**uckingham, **A**rlington, **L**auderdale. (Today they sound like whistle stops on a southeastern Amtrak route—but never mind.)

Let us investigate this conspiracy. Almost two centuries later, the famous historian Thomas Macaulay would call it "a whimsical coincidence." The word cabal derives from *cabala,* the school of occult mysticism discussed in the previous chapter. Beginning in the early seventeenth century, the word gradually acquired the sense of a sinister conspiracy by a small group. But although the ministers didn't invent the word, they did help to popularize it.

Speaking of cabala, **abracadabra** is said to originate from the Hebrew words **A**b (father), **B**en (son), and **R**uach **Hac**odesh (Holy Spirit). But this explanation is itself a bit mystical and doubtful. Although the precise etymology is unknown, some speculate that the word is from French by way of Greek, and in turn (perhaps) from Abraxas, the god of a third-century (current era) Gnostic sect in Alexandria. Others say it was first conjured up in the second century. The letters were written on parchment in the form of a pyramid, then placed in an amulet and worn as a charm, and believed thereby to cure illness and ward off dangers. It's appropriate that the origins of this venerable incantation of stage magicians should have such a mysterious past.

(Parental advisory: The following paragraphs are X-rated.)

Another spurious but endlessly repeated story claims that the familiar naughty word for sexual intercourse is from the phrase **f**or **u**nlawful **c**arnal **k**nowledge. Supposedly, this intimidating abbreviation was painted by our colonial ancestors on signs affixed to the stocks in which wrongdoers were punished, as a deterrent to others tempted to engage in such prohibited activities. In a variant account, the four-letter word was used on police blotters or by law clerks.

In an even wilder tale, an edict issued by Charles II (see above) during the Plague announced: "**F**ornicate **u**nder **c**ommand [or **c**onsent] of the **k**ing!" The objective of that peculiar ukase, presumably, was to replenish the decimated population.

All fascinating—and all wrong. Although the origin of the word is uncertain, one theory is that it is from the Middle English *firk* (a stroke or thrust, among other meanings), or from German *ficken* (ditto). Etymologists have speculated that the famous F word was borrowed from French, Latin, Greek, Swedish, or Norwegian. Despite all the conflicting accounts, the evidence is that it made its first recorded appearance in English (in the sense we know and love) in 1503, in a poem by William Dunbar, a Scot.

The preceding story would probably not be appreciated by a **wowser** (1890s), a term for a prudish reformer, bluenose, or killjoy, such as a missionary or a prohibitionist. Allegedly it's an acronym for the phrase "**w**e **o**nly **w**ant **s**ocial **e**vils **r**emedied [or **r**ighted]." Abandon ye those spirits of the devil, brother, and hearken unto this truth: According to *The Oxford English Dictionary,* wowser is (once again) "of obscure origin." But it was coined in Australia, and has been used in that part of the world to this day. John Norton, a Sydney newspaper editor, claimed (not convincingly) that he invented it. Other fanciful explanations are that it is from the reformer's cry "woe, sir!" or "whoa, sir!"

The word **camp**—in the colloquial sense of tacky,

tawdry, trendy, banal, exaggerated, outrageous, affected, or effeminate—is sometimes reported to be from an abbreviation used by the New York City Police Department: **k**nown **a**s **m**ale **p**rostitute, or **KAMP**. The true origin of the word (which is used as a noun, adjective, and verb) is not entirely clear, but it seems to date from the early twentieth century and has been variously identified as Australian or French, where it meant a homosexual, a brothel, or a saloon. Another explanation: In British dialect, camp refers to an impetuous or roguish fellow.

A **ham** (1919), in the sense of an amateur radio operator, has been said to derive from the name of a do-it-yourself magazine, ***H**ome **A**mateur **M**echanic,* or the call sign **H.A.M.**, allegedly from the initials of three college students who were the first radio amateurs. "The origin of the word is obscure," says Steve Mansfield, public information manager of the American Radio Relay League. "One theory holds that early amateur radio enthusiasts were called hams because they liked to 'perform' on the air, as in 'hamming it up.' Another theory proposes that the name came from the 'ham-fisted' way some early amateurs handled their code keys. The easiest opinion to accept is that 'ham' is a Briticism of 'am,' as in amateur."

Equally abounding in mythical lore are certain initialisms. For example, the letters **S.O.S.** did *not* originally mean "**S**ave **o**ur **s**hip!" (nor ". . . **s**ouls"). In 1908, the International Radio Telegraph Convention officially adopted these characters as a distress signal because the Morse code for the sequence (. . . . --- . . .) could be easily distinguished and rapidly transmitted.

Why do people invent explanations for the origins of words and spread old wives' tales such as these?

Scholars have speculated about the motives for folk etymology. Human beings, they say, want to feel at home with their language, so they devise comforting interpretations that coincide with their emotional needs. Also, acronymic explanations are colorful and easily comprehended—in contrast to the sometimes complex and tedious, if more accurate, histories proffered by etymologists and lexicographers.

According to Félix Rodríguez González, these fables are indicative of "a platonic mentality which tried to see in each word the acrostic of a phrase." (Well, what's wrong with that?) "Finding the real source of a word has spoiled many a clever story or pretty fantasy," ironically observes Sterling Eisiminger, a professor of English at Clemson University.

Although these yarns have been refuted many times, such plausible but inaccurate stories still find their way into dictionaries, books of word origins, and magazine and newspaper articles. People tend to assume that if something is "in print," it must be a fact.

Observes New York lexicographer Rob Schleifer: "I am always astonished at how so-called 'authorities' on words continue to make *and publish* the same silly etymological mistakes. But what I find even more astounding is that perhaps ninety percent of their mistakes could easily be avoided if only these experts were a little more conscientious and spent a few minutes cross-checking their etymologies with even one or two of our finer dictionaries."

Now you know. The next time you overhear people insisting that they have the "real meaning" of posh or cabal, you are prepared to set them straight and win all those bar bets.

Derivation and Compounding: Acronyms That Mutate

If they're not careful, drug addicts—oops! I should say "substance abusers"—might **O.D.** on L.S.D. This use of the common initialism for **o**ver**d**ose demonstrates that initialisms can function as verbs. So can acronyms.

Laser has given birth to the verb *to lase,* an instance (this one genuine) of *back-formation,* discussed earlier.

"Some verbs grow naturally out of military acronyms," noted the news magazine *Insight* during the 1991 Persian Gulf War. To prepare for incoming missiles, a soldier assumed a **m**ission-**o**riented **p**rotective **p**osture (donning chemical-resistant attire) and could answer in the affirmative when asked "Are you **MOPP**ed?" Similarly, **r**emain **o**ver**n**ight condenses to **RON**, which leads in turn to the verb —for example, "I'll be RONing in Bangkok." **RIF**, for **r**eduction **i**n **f**orce (a euphemism for getting fired) and the corresponding verb *to rif* (sometimes *riff*) in military and government use dates back at least to 1953. In the view of one writer, it intentionally evokes the word *rift.*

Len Deighton's 1962 novel *The Ipcress File* describes a British naval ship "NATOing down the Lebanese coastline." *Natoist* and *Natoism* are also used.

The cocktail party remark "She's Waspier than he is" proves that acronyms can also become adjectives. **Scuba** has generated compound forms such as *scuba diver, scuba equipment,* and so on. And consider *radar screen* and *radar-controlled, laser beam* and *laser-guided, yuppieish* and *yuppify.*

U.F.O. is an initialism, *not* an acronym. Nevertheless, when the term evolved into other forms, it was automatically acronymized—hence, *ufology* (presumably the study of unidentified flying objects) and *ufologist* (an authority on the subject). But the base becomes acronymic only temporarily. The term for the alien craft itself is never pronounced "you foe." And a good thing, too, if we earthlings ever experience a close encounter!

For decades, linguists have been debating the status of acronyms. Are they truly "words"—or something else?

Compelling evidence for the contention that acronyms have indeed acquired "lexical status" as genuine words is supplied by the fact that they can evolve from nouns into other forms and parts of speech, such as verbs and adjectives. Linguistic terms for this phenomenon include *derivation* and *inflection* (if the form of the word changes), and *conversion* or *functional shift* (if the word remains unchanged).

Like the often-cited duck, acronyms *act* like words, so they must *be* words.

They can also form compounds and gain affixes (prefixes and suffixes), as in pro-**NAFTA** (favoring the **N**orth **A**merican **F**ree **T**rade **A**greement) and **YAF**er (a member of **Y**oung **A**mericans for **F**reedom).

Acronyms and initialisms can even combine incestuously. **CAD/CAM** (**c**omputer-**a**ided **d**esign/**c**omputer-**a**ided **m**anufacturing) is a merger of two preexisting acronyms. **CD-ROM** (**c**ompact **d**isc-**r**ead **o**nly **m**emory) joins an initialism with an acronym. The banking industry initialisms **E.F.T.** (**e**lectronic **f**unds **t**ransfer) and **P.O.S.** (**p**oint **o**f **s**ale) have married to form **E.F.T./P.O.S.** *English Today* editor Tom McArthur has collected such abbreviated sets as **I.B.M. P.C.** and **Mr. T.V. Exec.**

Acronyms That Incorporate Acronyms

Speaking of compound forms, acronyms can spawn *other* acronyms, of which they are a component. On page 103 we noted the example of **pulsar** (in its hypothetical redefinition), which incorporates **laser**.

Laser is also part of **LOGIC** (**L**aser **O**ptical **G**uidance **I**ntegration **C**oncept) and **MILES** (**M**ultiple **I**ntegrated **L**aser **E**ngagement **S**ystem).

Radar has generated numerous "children." A small sampling: **ARSA** (**a**irport **r**adar **s**ervice **a**rea), **STARTLE** (**s**urveillance and **t**arget **a**cquisition **ra**dar for **t**ank **l**ocation and **e**ngagement), and **TRADE** (**t**racking **r**adar **a**ngle **d**eception **e**quipment).

Linguists call these "nested" or "embedded" acronyms. Word collector Paul Dickson refers to them as "second-generation acronyms." The process is potentially infinite: Acronyms that incorporate acronyms that incorporate acronyms!

This phenomenon serves as additional evidence that acronyms indeed function as words.

CHAPTER 5

❖

Causes, Organizations, Protests, Including Other Unusual Stuff (COPIOUS)

The specimens in this and the following chapter were carefully hand-selected after perusing hundreds of newspaper and magazine articles, reference volumes, and interview notes. I chose them because they struck me as apt, clever, or amusing. Not every organization is still around, but some were too good to omit.

These lists are by no means complete. If you need to find a specific acronym or its definition, consult a comprehensive dictionary of abbrevations, some of which are described in Appendix II.

Assorted Campaigns, Movements, and Causes

As we have noted, movements and groups advocating social change or some other agenda often seek a name that communicates its purpose or mission, stimulates interest, and builds support. An acronymic name may be chosen to fit an appropriate word, or a word might happen to fit the name.

Among the more tendentious examples:

HALT, **H**elp **A**bolish **L**egal **T**yranny, a law reform organization

ROAR, **R**estore **O**ur **A**lienated **R**ights, a Boston antibusing group

CAUTION, **C**itizens **A**gainst **U**nnecessary **T**ax **I**ncreases and **O**ther **N**onsense, a St. Louis group that in 1971 fought a bond issue for a convention center

SET, **S**ociety for the **E**radication of **T**elevision; they're serious!

SCORN, **S**pecial **C**ommittee **O**pposing **R**esurgent **N**azism

CAUSTIC, **C**ampaign **A**gainst **U**nnecessary **S**exist **T**erminology **i**n **C**hemistry

PEACE, **P**eople **E**merging **A**gainst **C**orrupt **E**stablishments, an underground military newspaper

CAFCA, **C**itizens **A**gainst **F**oreign **C**ontrol **o**f **A**merica ("Cafca-esque"?)

SCROD, **S**pecial **C**ommittee to **R**estore the **O**gunquit **D**unes, a group opposing construction of a dike in Maine; for a fish story about *scrod,* see page 116

CRASH, **C**itizens to **R**estrict **A**irline **S**moking **H**azards

FLAAG, **F**ederated **L**eague of **A**mericans **A**round the **G**lobe

SCRAM, **S**cottish **C**ampaign to **R**esist the **A**tomic **M**enace

FLAME, **F**acts and **L**ogic **A**bout the **M**iddle **E**ast

In Chapter 1 we noted the phenomenon of duplication. Occasionally several groups have the same idea. For example:

FREE is the **F**und to **R**estore an **E**ducated **E**lectorate, **F**oundation for **R**ational **E**conomics and **E**ducation, **F**riends of **R**efugees of **E**astern **E**urope, **F**ellowship for **R**acial and **E**conomic **E**quality (later changed to Southeast Institute), and others.

HOPE is the hospital ship U.S.S. *HOPE,* which means **H**ealth **O**pportunity for **P**eople **E**verywhere, plus **H**ousing **O**ur **P**eople **E**conomically, **H**elp **O**bese **P**eople **E**verywhere, and others.

POWER is **P**eople **O**rganized and **W**orking for **E**conomic **R**ebirth (subsequently changed), **P**rofessionals **O**rganized for **W**omen's **E**qual **R**ights, **P**romote **O**ur **W**onderful **E**nergy **R**esources, and more.

SAVE is **S**tudent **A**ction **V**oters for **E**cology, **S**top **A**ddiction through **V**oluntary **E**ffort, and **S**hoppers **A**ssociation for **V**alue **E**conomy.

Opponents of Sex Education

Among the groups (wowsers?) who object to their kids being taught about sexual matters:

MOMS, **Mo**thers for **M**oral **S**tability

POPS, **P**arents **O**pposed to **P**ornography in **S**chools

PAUSE, **P**eople **A**gainst **U**nconstitutional **S**ex **E**d-ucation

POSSE, **P**arents **O**pposed to **S**ex and **S**ensitivity **E**ducation

POPE, **P**arents for **O**rthodoxy in **P**arochial **E**du-cation

MOTOREDE, **Mo**vement **to Re**store **De**cency

Feminists and Others

Women's **H**ealth **A**nd **M**obilization, a New York City pro-choice group, is emphatically **WHAM**! **W**omen **A**gainst **R**ape have declared **WAR**.

NOW (**N**ational **O**rganization for **W**omen) in-spired the *anti*feminist **THEN** (**T**hose **H**ags **E**n-courage **N**euterism).

On opposite sides are **RASP** (**R**esidents **A**gainst **S**treet **P**rostitution), a New York City group, and **WHISPER** (**W**omen **H**urt **i**n **S**ystems of **P**rostitu-tion **E**ngaged in **R**evolt), Detroit.

More extreme feminists are members of **SCUM** (**S**ociety for **C**utting **U**p **M**en) and **WITCH** (**W**omen's **I**nternational **T**errorist **C**onspiracy from **H**ell). On campus, **WITCH** is also **W**omen **I**ncensed over **T**raditional **C**oed **H**oopla.

Less radical people may join **LADIES** (**L**ife **A**fter **D**ivorce **I**s **E**ventually **S**ane), **OWL** (**O**lder **W**omen's **L**eague), and **LAW** (**L**adies **A**gainst **W**omen), whose stated goals appear to suggest that they are not entirely serious.

Males have not been idle, striking back with **ADAM** (**A**merican **D**ivorce **A**ssociation of **M**en), **HAWK** (**H**ave **A**limony, **W**ill **K**eep), **WORMS** (**W**orld **O**rganization to **R**estore **M**ale **S**upremacy), and **MACHO** (**M**en **A**llied to **C**ombat **H**ypocrisy and **O**ppression).

Student Legal Action Groups

These are groups of law students, under the direction of a professor, working toward politically correct social reform.

SCRAP, **S**tudents **C**hallenging **R**egulatory **A**gency **P**rocedures

SLICE, **S**tudents **L**itigating **I**njurious **C**an **E**dges

SMASH, **S**tudents **M**obilizing on **A**uto **S**afety **H**azards

SHOCK, **S**tudents **H**ot **o**n **C**onserving **K**ilowatts

FATS, **F**ight to **A**dvertise the **T**ruth about **S**aturates

BUS STOP, **B**reathers **U**nited to **S**top **S**tanding **T**ime **o**f **P**assenger Buses

SNOOP, **S**tudents **N**aturally **O**pposed to **O**utrageous **P**rying

MEDIA, **M**ove to **E**nd **D**eception **i**n **A**dvertising

VIOLENT, **V**iewers **I**ntent **o**n **L**isting Violent **E**pisodes on **N**ational **T**elevision

RIGHTS, **R**eforming **I**nstitutions to **G**uarantee **H**umane **T**reatment **S**tandards

Share (their typography), **S**tudents **H**ave **a** **R**esponsibility **E**verywhere

Meanwhile, companies convinced that they are being unfairly targeted by consumer groups are hitting back with **SLAPP**s. These **s**trategic **l**awsuits **a**gainst **p**ublic **p**articipation charge opponents with libel, defamation, or interference with business.

In the 1960s, the proliferation of student groups inspired the facetious **SPASM** (**S**ociety for the **P**revention of **A**sinine **S**tudent **M**ovements) and **SWINE** (**S**tudents **W**ildly **I**ndignant about **N**early **E**verything), a creation of "L'il Abner" cartoonist Al Capp.

During the 1991 Persian Gulf War, college campuses witnessed **SMASH** (**S**tudents **M**obilized **A**gainst **S**addam **H**ussein), whose members denounced **SCUD** (**S**adly **C**onfused **U**npatriotic **D**emonstrators).

Local and Neighborhood Causes

The cry of "**N**ot **i**n **m**y **b**ackyard!," or **NIMBY**, has become a universal protest slogan of citizens opposed to the establishment in their neighborhoods of prisons, homeless shelters, incinerators, and so forth.

What galvanized them into action? None other than **LULU**, or **l**ocally **u**ndesirable **l**and **u**se. In one Manhattan neighborhood, residents outraged at the burdens imposed on them by such facilities formed a group called **B**efore **A**nother **S**helter **T**ears Us **A**part, or **BASTA.** In both Spanish and Italian, *basta* means "enough!"

In both the United States and the United Kingdom, a protester against unwanted neighborhood construction is called *a nimby,* with *a nimby attitude,* who supports *nimbyism.* Other "Not in my . . ." formulations pop up from time to time.

Other local groups:

RAGE-ON!, **R**evolt **A**gainst **G**entrification **E**rasing **O**ur **N**eighborhood, in New York City's East Village

SSSH!, **S**ociety for **S**ilent **S**nowmobiles **H**ere, Pontiac, Michigan

BUSWREC, **B**an **U**nsafe **S**choolbuses **W**hich **R**egularly **E**ndanger **C**hildren

CAN DO, **C**hicago **A**ssociation of **N**eighborhood **D**evelopment **O**rganizations

Fashion Protests

In the early 1970s, the lower hemlines of midi- and maxi-apparel sparked a wave of tongue-in-cheek protest movements:

SMACK, **S**ociety of **M**ales who **A**ppreciate **C**ute **K**nees

FADD, **F**ight **A**gainst **D**ictating **D**esigners, Washington, D.C.

STEMS, **S**ociety **t**o **E**ncourage **M**ini**s**kirts

OGLE, **O**rganization for **G**etting **L**egs **E**xposed

PEEK, **P**eople for the **E**njoyment of **E**yeballing **K**nees

MOXIE, **M**en **O**rganized to **X**-press **I**ndignant **E**xasperation, Seattle (*moxie,* a slang term for courage, came from the brand name of a soft drink, no longer manufactured but popular in New England beginning about 1930)

GAMS, **G**irls/**G**uys **A**gainst **M**ore **S**kirt, New York City

MAMMA, **M**en **A**gainst the **M**axi-**M**idi **A**trocity, Switzerland

WHIM, **W**omen **H**appy **in** **M**inis, Boise

The inevitable reaction was the formation of **SPOOFF**, **S**ociety for the **P**rogress **of** **O**ur **F**eminine **F**ashions, a whimsical Los Angeles defense of the new styles. We can't omit **FOOTS**, **F**emale **O**rganization **O**pposing **T**orturous **S**hoes.

Ecology and Environment

NOSE (**N**eighbors **O**pposing **S**melly **E**missions) is a student legal action group. A Washington, D.C., organization had a similar idea: **N**eighbors **O**rganized for **S**tench **E**limination. Among others:

GOO, **G**et **O**il **O**ut! Residents of Santa Barbara, Calif., fighting drilling platforms that caused massive leaks in 1969

YUK, **Y**outh **U**ncovering **K**rud

YES, **Y**outh for **E**nvironmental **S**anity

LIFE, **L**et's **I**mprove **F**uture **E**nvironment

HOW, **H**elp **O**ur **W**orld

STOP, **S**tudents **T**ackle **O**cean **P**lastics

AMPS, **A**mericans for **M**ore **P**ower **S**ources

SAFE, **S**tudents **A**cting for the **F**uture of the **E**arth

CHOKE, **C**are **H**ow **O**thers **K**eep the **E**nvironment

LEAF, **L**adies **E**nvironmentally **A**ware of **F**orests, Australia

NOPE, **N**ot **o**n **P**lanet **E**arth, which opposes dangerous wastes

WALRUS, **W**ater **a**nd **L**and **R**esources **U**se **S**imulation

WARP, **W**oodworkers **A**ssociation for **R**ainforest **P**rotection

CAGE, **C**onvicts' **A**ssociation for a **G**ood **E**nvironment

Other Organizational Onomastics

Onomastics, the study of proper names, gives us an attractively alliterative appellation for this section.

Having decided on a name, an organization may find that it forms an initialism. Or the name may create a meaningless acronym such as **ASCAP** (**A**merican **S**ociety for **C**omposers, **A**uthors, and **P**ublishers) or **UNESCO** (**U**nited **N**ations **E**ducational, **S**cientific, and **C**ultural **O**rganization).

But many organizational acronyms are singularly well suited to their purposes. Consider, for example, the federal **A**gency for **I**nternational **D**evelopment (**AID**), **V**olunteers **i**n **S**ervice **t**o **A**merica (**VISTA**), and **A**merican **C**ouncil **t**o **I**mprove **O**ur **N**eighborhoods (**ACTION,** changed to National Urban Coalition).

Women **i**n **L**ivestock **D**evelopment, we assume, are **WILD**, while **G**orgeous **L**adies **o**f **W**restling presumably **GLOW**. Meanwhile, the Manassas, Va.-based **M**others' **A**ccess **t**o **C**areers at **H**ome seeks to **MATCH** women who work while raising children.

A support organization for people who are widowed is called **T**hey **H**elp **E**ach **O**ther **S**piritually, or **THEOS** (Greek for *God*). **P**eople **A**gainst **C**ult **T**herapy have evidently formed a **PACT**. Members of the **S**ociety for the **P**reservation of **E**nglish **L**anguage and **L**iterature can certainly **SPELL**.

The **C**enter for **U**nderstanding the **B**uilt **E**nvironment (**CUBE**) teaches kids about architecture. They might have enjoyed a visit from the **N**ational **A**ssociation of **I**ndependent **L**umbermen (**NAIL**), but this group is, unfortunately, defunct.

Among other apposite group names:

WAIF, **W**orld **A**doption **I**nternational **F**und

CAMERA, **C**ommittee for **A**ccuracy in **M**iddle **E**ast **R**eporting in **A**merica

ACORN, **A**ssociation of **C**ommunity **O**rganizations for **R**eform **N**ow

CRUCIAL, **C**oalition for the **R**econstruction of **U**nited **C**ommunity **I**nvolvement **a**nd **L**eadership

PLASMA, **P**arents' **L**eague of **A**merican **S**tudents of **M**edicine **A**broad

STRIVE, **S**tudents **T**aking **R**eal **I**nitiative for **V**ocational **E**xcellence

CANDLES, **C**hildren of **A**uschwitz-**N**azis' **D**eadly **L**ab **E**xperiments **S**urvivors

WOMAN, **W**orld **O**rganization of **M**others of **A**ll **N**ations

SCRAP, **S**crounger's **C**enter for **R**e-usable **A**rt **P**arts, a San Francisco organization that accepts donations of materials for schools and community programs

VOCAL, **V**ictims **o**f **C**hild **A**buse **L**aws

VOICE, **V**ictims **o**f **I**ncest **C**an **E**merge

Motivating and inspiring names include **HUMAN** (**H**elp **U**s **M**ake **a** **N**ation), **HURRAH** (**H**elp **U**s **R**each and **R**ehabilitate **A**merica's **H**andicapped), and **REACH** (**R**esponsible, **E**ducated **A**dolescents **C**an **H**elp).

Animal lovers can find their pet cause among:

CATS, **C**are **A**bout **t**he **S**trays

WHOA, **W**alking **H**orse **O**wner's **A**ssociation

WHOA!, **W**ild **H**orse **O**rganized **A**ssistance

MASH, **M**issourians **A**gainst **S**laughtering **H**orses

SAFE, **S**ave **A**nimals **f**rom **E**xtinction

FAWN, **F**riends **A**ware of **W**ildlife **N**eeds

HOWL, **H**elp **O**ur **W**olves **L**ive

HARE, **H**umans **A**gainst **R**abbit **E**xploitation

These groups might not support **A**nimal **R**esearch **F**acilities (**ARF**) but may be interested in **P**ets **A**re **W**orth **S**afeguarding (**PAWS**) or **P**ets **A**re **W**onderful (**PAW**), the latter a 1981 advertising campaign by the pet food industry to encourage people to adopt "animal companions."

Action on **S**moking and **H**ealth (**ASH**) wants to snuff out every cigarette, while **G**roup **A**gainst **S**mokers' **P**ollution (**GASP**) seeks to abolish coughing. The Watertown, Mass.-based **P**arents **A**gainst **S**econdhand **S**moke, concerned about their children's health, petitions judges in custody disputes to **PASS** up estranged spouses who use the evil weed. A previously cited group of physicians (and others) opposed to smoking is called **D**octors **O**ught to **C**are, or **DOC**. **SHAME** says it's the **S**ociety to **H**umiliate, **A**ggravate, **M**ortify, and **E**mbarrass

Smokers—but omits the last word from its acronym.

Meanwhile, smokers' rights groups are striking back with the **C**ommittee **I**nsuring and **G**uaranteeing **A**nyone's **R**ight to **S**moke (**CIGARS**), **P**eople **U**nited **f**or **F**riendly **S**moking (**PUFFS**), and, in London, **F**reedom **O**rganization for the **R**ight to **E**njoy **S**moking **T**obacco (**FOREST**).

Drug rehabilitation groups include:

HAVEN, **H**elp **A**ddicts **V**oluntarily **E**nd **N**arcotics

BABES, **B**eginning **A**lcohol and **A**ddictions **B**asic **E**ducation **S**tudies, Detroit

DARE, **D**rug **A**buse **R**esistance **E**ducation, *and* **D**rug and **A**lcohol **R**ehabilitation and **E**ducation

CARES, **C**hemical **A**buse **R**educed through **E**ducation and **S**ervices

DAWN, **D**rug **A**buse **W**arning **N**etwork, a federal project

PRIDE, **P**arents **R**esource **I**nstitute for **D**rug **E**ducation, Atlanta

KIND, **K**ids **i**n **N**eed of **D**irection

TIP, **T**urn **i**n a **P**usher

Meanwhile, some people prefer to mobilize in favor of the decriminalization of drugs. Perhaps the best known is the **N**ational **O**rganization to **R**eform **M**arijuana **L**aws (**NORML**). Others are **H**elp **E**nd **M**arijuana **P**rohibition (**HEMP**), **B**asic **L**iberation **o**f **S**mokers and **S**ympathizers **o**f **M**arijuana (**BLOSSOM**), and **St**udent **A**ssociation for the **S**tudy of **H**allucinogens (**STASH**, now defunct). In California, state officials are fighting back with their **C**ampaign **A**gainst **M**arijuana **P**lanting (**CAMP**).

Social Service Groups

JOB is **J**ust **O**ne **B**reak, founded in 1947 to obtain employment for disabled people. **JOBS** is **J**ob **O**pportunities and **B**asic **S**kills, a Detroit training program. Among other groups:

LIFE, **L**ove **I**s **F**eeding **E**verybody

FOCUS, **F**riends **O**ffering **C**hallenge, **U**nderstanding and **S**ervice

SWIM, **S**aturation **W**ork **I**nitiative **M**odel, a successful San Diego program that finds jobs for welfare recipients ("Sink or SWIM"?)

FAMILY, **F**athers **a**nd **M**others **i**n **L**eague with **Y**outh, Detroit

KENNY, **K**ids **E**verywhere **N**ow **N**eed **Y**ou (named for Timothy M. Kenny, a Michigan prosecutor)

WARM, **W**eatherization **a**nd **R**etrofit **M**aintenance

Groups helping people learn to read or to read better include **P**ush **L**iteracy **A**ction **N**ow (**PLAN**); **P**roject **L**iteracy **US** (**PLUS**), a joint venture of ABC and PBS; and **S**earch for **E**ducation, **E**levation, and **K**nowledge (**SEEK**), a City University of New York remedial program.

MADD (**M**others **A**gainst **D**runk **D**riving) inspired **DAMM** (**D**runks **A**gainst **M**ad **M**others), which was coined, presumably in jest, by redneck movie reviewer "Joe Bob Briggs" (John Bloom). Predictably, the moms were MADD, not amused. The success of that group inspired:

SADD, **S**tudents **A**gainst **D**runk **D**riving

DADD, **D**ealers **A**gainst **D**runk **D**riving, Washington, D.C., auto retailers

BADD, **B**artenders **A**gainst **D**runk **D**riving, *and* **B**usiness **A**gainst **D**runk **D**riving

RID, **R**emove **I**ntoxicated **D**rivers

CRASH, **C**ountermeasures **R**elated to **A**lcohol and **S**afety on the **H**ighways

Affinity Groups

Aptly named professional organizations include **P**overty **L**awyers for **E**ffective **A**dvocacy (**PLEA**), **H**orror/**O**ccult **W**riters **L**eague (**HOWL**), **T**ubists **U**niversal **B**rotherhood **A**ssociation (**TUBA**), and the **N**etwork of **A**merican **N**anny **A**gencies (**NANA**).

PIPE is the **P**lumbing **I**ndustry **P**rogress and **E**ducation Fund, and **SEA** is the **S**afety **E**quipment **A**ssociation, a trade group of marine manufacturers.

Hobbyist associations can be acronymic, too.

Zymurgists have the last word—at least in many dictionaries! While cooking up their own beer, they display a sense of humor, as indicated by New Jersey's **M**id-**A**tlantic **S**udsers and **H**oppers (**MASH**); **B**rewers **U**nited for **R**eal **P**otables (**BURP**) in the Washington, D.C., area; **P**aumanok **U**nited **B**rewers (**PUB**) in Long Island, N.Y.; and **T**hree **R**ivers **A**lliance of **S**erious **H**omebrewers (**TRASH**), in Pittsburgh. One hopes that they don't **f**eel **l**ike **a** **b**eer (**FLAB**) too often!

Really Unusual Groups

Let's conclude this chapter with a list of organizations so specialized and eccentric, and equipped with acronymic names so silly, that you might assume they are fictitious. But however risible the names might appear, the groups are real. I think.

(A few seem to like periods, and we shall respect their style.)

N.O.T.S.A.F.E. is the **N**ational **O**rganization **T**aunting **S**afety **a**nd **F**airness **E**verywhere, a Montecito, Calif.-based group that pokes fun at excessive government regulation.

INATAPROBU, the **In**ter**nat**ional **A**ssociation of **Pro**fessional **Bu**reaucrats, lampoons governmental gobbledegook and is based (where else?) in Washington, D.C.

RALPH was the **R**oyal **A**ssociation for the **L**ongevity and **P**reservation of *The **H**oneymooners.* "Having achieved all our goals," says co-founder Bob Columbe, "we are no longer an active membership organization."

SCROOGE is the **S**ociety to **C**urtail **R**idiculous, **O**utrageous, and **O**stentatious **G**ift **E**xchange. Based in Charlottesville, Va., it protests Christmas commercialism.

SPERM, the **S**ociety for the **P**rotection and **E**ncouragement of **R**ighteous **M**anhood, is a discussion group for males. Sam Keen, best-selling author of *Fire in the Belly,* is a former member.

Presumably unrelated is **S.P.E.R.M.F.L.O.W.**, the **S**ociety for the **P**reservation and **E**nhancement of the **R**ecognition of **M**illard **F**illmore, **L**ast **o**f the **W**higs. From Cascade, Colo., the group is "dedicated to the celebration of mediocrity in American culture, as epitomized by Millard Fillmore."

COYOTE, **C**all **O**ff **Y**our **O**ld **T**ired **E**thics, is the former (but still used) name of the San Francisco-based National Task Force on Prostitution. It's a coalition of groups devoted to the rights of what were once known as ladies of the evening (now therapeutic sexual surrogates). **PONY** is **P**rostitutes **o**f **N**ew **Y**ork; **CAT** is the **C**alifornia **A**ssociation of **T**rollops.

BLOOP is the **B**enevolent and **L**oyal **O**rder **o**f **P**essimists. Based in Iowa City, it was "founded to counteract the insidious spread of optimists' clubs."

CURSE is the **C**ommittee **U**nited to **R**evive **S**treaking **E**vents.

RESISTORS, a neat double pun, stands for **R**adically **E**mphatic **S**tudents **I**nterested in **S**cience, **T**echnology and **O**ther **R**esearch **S**tudies.

GASGASGAS, a trade group, is the **G**ild of **A**ncient **S**uppliers of **G**as **A**ppliances, **S**kills, **G**ins, **A**ccessories, and **S**ubstances.

BUFF was **B**each **U**sers **f**or **F**reedom, and **BARE**, **B**eaches **A**re **R**eally **E**veryone's. As you might guess, they promoted nude sunbathing. Sadly (for the cause of acronyms), both are now defunct.

C**orrespondents **o**f the **W**orld **A**gainst **B**eancounting and **U**njust **G**utting of **A**llowances!*, or ***COWABUNGA!, is the name of a publication produced by some *Wall Street Journal* overseas reporters protesting pay cuts.

For anyone under the age of forty, "cowabunga!" (originally "kawabonga!," if it matters), was the jubilant cry of the Indian chief on *Howdy Doody* in the early 1950s. The "word" was invented by Eddie Kean, a *Howdy* writer. More recently, it has been adopted by surfers and Ninja Turtles. (Note: Stereotypes of Native Americans are now politically incorrect.)

We suspect that the teachers' organization called **G**eriatric **O**rder of **O**ld **D**olls who **E**ncourage the **G**eneration **G**ap **S**inglemindedly (**GOOD EGGS**), and the **H**onorary **O**rder of **T**rumpeters **L**iving **i**n **P**ossible **S**in (**HOTLIPS**) are tongue-in-cheek. But who knows?

CHAPTER 6

Gosh! Really Elegant Acronyms Touch All Professions, Every Specialty! (GREAT APES)

Each field and discipline evolves its own terminology. Some of this specialized language is in the form of initialisms, acronyms, or other abbreviations. Here are selected examples.

Medicine and Psychology

The motives for abbreviation in technical fields are practical: to condense long and cumbersome terms. But as noted earlier, some cynics claim the purposes are more sinister: to create an impenetrable "insider" jargon that restricts knowledge to an elite brotherhood and conceals it from outsiders.

This charge is perhaps most vehemently directed against medicine. True or false? You be the judge.

Not all professional argot is of equal interest to us. Medicine is filled with run-of-the-mill initialisms: **E.E.G.**, **E.K.G.**, **M.R.I.**, **T.I.A.**, and so on.

Some terms form acronyms that are not especially apt, such as **TENS** for **t**ranscutaneous **e**lectrical **n**erve **s**timulation. Others we scornfully dismiss as "pseudo-acronyms," such as the previously cited **C.A.B.G.** for **c**oronary **a**rtery **b**ypass **g**raft, which cardiac surgeons pronounce "cabbage."

The multisyllabic acronymic names of pharmaceuticals are usually not very appealing, such as **sulfanilamide** (from **sulf**uric, **anil**ine, **am**monia), **ibuprofen** (iso-**bu**tyl **pro**pionic **phen**yl), and **L-dopa** (levo-**dio**xy**p**henyl**a**lanine).

The names of a few drugs denote their origins. For example, **warfarin** was coined from **WARF** (**W**isconsin **A**lumni **R**esearch **F**oundation), where it was discovered in 1950, and the suffix of coum**arin.** A versatile drug, warfarin functions both as an anticoagulant medication and as a rat poison.

A steroid compound called hydroxydeoxycorticosterone is perhaps appropriately truncated to **OH-DOC.** This tricky acronym requires some explanation. The **O** is for oxygen, the **H** for hydrogen—which elements together constitute the **hydroxy** prefix. **DOC** is obtained from key letters of **de**o**x**y-**c**orticosterone.

Some pathogens and ailments are acronymic. The rather innocent-sounding **echo**virus is a potentially dangerous gastrointestinal bug, short for **e**nteric **c**ytopathogenic **h**uman **o**rphan virus. **C**hronic **o**bstructive **l**ung **d**isease is **COLD**.

A few other medical acronyms:

CAT scan, **c**omputerized **a**xial **t**omography

PET scan, **p**ositron **e**mission **t**omography

GIFT, **g**amete **i**ntra-**f**allopian **t**ransfer—an appropriate name for the goal of infertile couples eagerly seeking a child

SWIFT is the query "**S**hould **w**e **i**ntervene **f**ollowing **t**hrombolysis?"

Medical organizations:

PAIN, **P**an-**A**merican **I**nstitute of **N**eurology

HEAL, **H**ealth **E**ducation **A**uthority of **L**ouisiana

BRAIN, **B**asic **R**egional **A**dvocacy **I**nformation **N**etwork, a Florida coalition of mental health groups

CORNEA, **C**onsortium **o**f **R**egistered **N**urses for **E**ye **A**cquisition

ASSERT, **A**ustralian **S**ociety of **S**exual **E**ducators, **R**esearchers, and **T**herapists

FEED, **F**oundation for **E**ducation about **E**ating **D**isorders

Also appropriately named are **PEP**, for **P**harmacological **E**rection **P**rogram, and **ROMP**, for **R**ecovery **o**f **M**ale **P**otency, a chain of clinics that treat impotence.

Some medical initialisms and acronyms are euphemisms designed to avoid alarming patients and visitors. Such expressions may, however, achieve the opposite effect, as when a patient overheard his attending physician say **S.O.B.** for **s**hortness **o**f **b**reath.

Medical abbreviations can display a humorous and sometimes macabre touch. A patient who is comatose or who has a mysterious ailment is a **GORK** (**G**od **o**nly **r**eally **k**nows). Previously **GOK,** it's been around since the early 1900s.

A patient can also be labeled a **GOMER**, often explained as an acronym for "**G**et **o**ut of **m**y **e**mergency **r**oom!" It's not as cruel as it sounds, though. The term refers to a chronically complaining patient, usually male, older, and disheveled (formerly known as a derelict), who checks into a hospital because it's a comfortable place to stay for a while. Such malingerers occupy the time and attention of doctors, taking them away from serious cases. Some researchers question the purported acronymic origin of GOMER. Other suggested etymologics include the T.V. character Gomer Pyle, a contraction of *go-homer,* and alleged provenances in Scottish dialect, modern Hebrew, and even the Bible. The GOMER's distaff (and somewhat more respectable) cousin is the **LOL** in **NAD** (**l**ittle **o**ld **l**ady in **n**o **a**pparent **d**istress).

One hopes that physicians don't read **CASH** (**c**hronic **a**ddiction **s**erum **h**epatitis) too literally. For some facetious medical acronyms, see page 223.

As we noted in Chapter 1, if medical jargon and abbreviations are not understood—or are misunderstood—the consequences might be serious. Consider the notorious penmanship skills of some physicians.

Any patient would likely be terrified by an article that appeared in a journal for nurses, accompanied by a handy list of medical abbreviations with ambiguous meanings. A doctor's hastily scrawled **o.d.**, meaning **o**nce **d**aily, is frequently misinterpreted as **OD**, for *oculus dexter.* As a result, the article helpfully points out, "oral medication is [inadvertently] administered in a patient's right eye." Oops! Fortunately, a writer in the magazine *Hippocrates* reassures us that "death by abbreviation is relatively rare."

One medical acronym that has become regrettably familiar is **AIDS**, for **A**cquired **I**mmune **D**eficiency **S**yndrome. The term was coined at the Centers for Disease Control in 1982. Prior to that, AIDS was called **GRID**, for **G**ay-**R**elated **I**mmune **D**eficiency.

British language commentator Philip Howard observes that AIDS "sounds rather friendly, and creates confusion with a number of other similar words." Indeed, some institutions have reportedly stopped using the word aids (or aides) for helpers or trainees. Market researchers now prefer to say "health and beauty *care.*" A software company called Advanced Information and Decision Systems decided to change its name. The diet candy named

Ayds, no longer manufactured, may have been a casualty.

The epidemic has inspired the creation of numerous organizations whose acronymic names incorporate an acronym. Perhaps the most visible is **ACT-UP**, the **A**IDS **C**oalition **t**o **U**nleash **P**ower. **HEAL** is the **H**ealth **E**ducation **A**IDS **L**iaison. **DREAM** consists of **D**ancers **R**esponding **E**agerly to the **A**IDS **M**ission.

Although the component words were reordered, in Spanish, French, and Italian, the acronym for AIDS is the same: **SIDA**.

Names of diet and health programs are often inspirational:

TOPS, **T**ake **O**ff **P**ounds **S**ensibly

ERASE, **E**at **R**ight **a**nd **S**lim **E**asily

ESTEEM, **E**mpower **S**elf **T**hrough **E**ducation and **E**ating **M**anagement

REACH, **R**espond **E**arly **a**nd **C**ontrol **H**ypertension

W.E.T., **W**ater **E**xercise **T**echnique, which became a book called *The W.E.T. Workout*

The cutest such acronym may be **MR FIT**, for **M**ultiple **R**isk **F**actor **I**ntervention **T**rial, a long-term study of the health habits of Americans.

In psychology, depressed people who suffer from **s**easonal **a**ffective **d**isorder are, not surprisingly,

SAD. For some patients, **f**alse **e**vidence **a**ppearing **r**eal inspires **FEAR**. **H**igher-**o**rder **t**hinking **s**kills presumably give you the **HOTS**. And **p**ornography **r**esearch **u**sing **d**irect **e**rotic **s**timuli is **PRUDES**. Mnemonic formulas are also popular. An Australian psychologist suggests that athletes can **COPE** with stress by "**c**ontrolling emotions, **o**rganizing input, **p**lanning the subsequent responses, and **e**xecuting appropriate actions."

Steven L. Baggish, a Connecticut psychotherapist, counsels his patients, when they experience **GUILT**, to **g**ive **u**p **i**rrational **l**eftover **t**houghts. He says it works!

Computers

The personal computer has generated a raft of new terminology, familiar to every user: **RAM** and **ROM**, **GUI** and **WYSIWYG**, **WORM** and **LAN**, **ASCII** and **modem**.

The term **bit** (**bi**nary digi**t**) led to **byte** (said to be coined from "**bi**nary digi**t** **e**ight"). **MIPS** is **mi**llions of **i**nstructions **p**er **s**econd, and **FLOPS** is **fl**oating-point **o**perations **p**er **s**econd.

Many micro and mainframe computer languages bear syllabic acronym names, such as **FORTRAN** (**For**mula **Tran**slation), **COBOL** (**Co**mmon **B**usiness-**O**riented **L**anguage—or sometimes "**c**ompiles **o**nly **b**ecause **o**f **l**uck"), and the rather convoluted **SNOBOL** (**S**tri**n**g-**O**riented Sym**bo**lic **L**anguage). **BASIC**, however, is a conventional letter acronym

(**B**eginner's **A**ll-Purpose **S**ymbolic **I**nstruction **C**ode). An artificial intelligence language developed for medical computing is **MUMPS** (**M**assachusetts General Hospital **U**tility **M**ulti**p**rogramming **S**ystem).

When I began using my computer to "spool-print," I didn't know **SPOOL** was an acronym for **s**imultaneous **p**eripheral **o**peration **o**n-**l**ine. The term **abend** (often lower-cased) is the **ab**normal **end** of an operation. *Abend* is German for evening, suggesting a pun on when such problems are likely to occur.

Some coinages are so profound and evocative that they have become part of the language of noncomputer users, such as **GIGO** (**g**arbage **i**n, **g**arbage **o**ut).

But computer acronyms are by no means a recent development. The predecessor of the modern computer, created for the Army at the University of Pennsylvania in 1946, was called **ENIAC**, for **E**lectronic **N**umerical **I**ntegrator **a**nd **C**alculator. Although the acronym was meaningless, the suffix caught on. **EDVAC** (**E**lectronic **D**iscrete **Va**riable **C**omputer) was completed in 1952, and **EDSAC** (**E**lectronic **D**elay **S**torage **A**utomatic **C**omputer) in 1949. Not exactly an acronym but clearly echoing the pattern, **JOHNNIAC** was named for mathematician John von Neumann. **UNIVAC** (**Univ**ersal **A**utomatic **C**omputer), introduced in 1951, was the first commercial computer, and became enormously successful.

The **-IAC** formula is no longer used, and already sounds archaic. The trend may have ended due to the model infelicitously named the **M**athematical **A**nalyzer, **N**umerator, **I**ntegrator, **a**nd **C**omputer, or **MANIAC**.

More fetchingly named machines include **EUCLID**, for **E**xperimental **U**se **C**omputer—**L**ondon **I**ntegrated **D**isplay, and **CHILD**, alternatively **C**omputer **H**aving **I**ntelligent **L**earning and **D**evelopment, *and* **C**ognitive **H**ybrid **I**ntelligent **L**earning **D**evice.

One especially appealing name is **RUNCIBLE**, for **R**evised **U**nified **N**ew **C**omputer with **I**ts **B**asic **L**anguage **E**xtended. It was borrowed from Edward Lear's nonsense word in "The Owl and the Pussycat." One line of the poem reads: "They dined on mince, and slices of quince,/Which they ate with a runcible spoon." Although Lear neglected to supply a definition for his 1871 coinage, it later came to mean a curved fork with three broad tines, one sharp. The word is in dictionaries.

A spirit of fun is also evident in:

MOUTH, **M**odular **O**utput **U**nit for **T**alking to **H**umans

PARTNER, **P**roof of **A**nalog **R**esults **T**hrough a **N**umerical **E**quivalent **R**outine

CONCISE, **C**omputer-**O**riented **N**otation **C**oncerning **I**nfrared **S**pectral **E**valuation, a programming language in analytical chemistry

BICEPS, **B**asic **I**ndustrial **C**ontrol **E**ngineering **P**rogramming **S**ystem

MASCOT, **M**odern **A**pproach to **S**oftware **C**onstruction, **O**peration and **T**est, a project of the British Ministry of Defence

BRAINS, **B**ehavior **R**eplication by **A**nalog **In**struction of the **N**ervous **S**ystem

THE BRAIN, **T**he **H**arvard **E**xperimental **B**asic **R**eckoning **a**nd **I**nstructional **N**etwork

I performed most of the research for this book at New York's Forty-second Street Library, where the computerized cataloging system is called **CATNYP** (**Cat**alog of the **N**ew **Y**ork **P**ublic Library), and at New York University's Bobst Library, which has its **BOBCAT**—a pun on both the benefactor for whom the building is named and the school's mascot.

In 1986, the Library of Congress announced a contest to name its new computer system. Among the two hundred or so entries received were **LASSO** (**L**ibrary **A**cquisition **S**ervices **S**ystem **O**n-Line), **SNOOPI** (**S**ystem **N**etwork **O**n-Line **Op**erations **I**nformation), and **PIGLET** (**P**urchase **I**nformation, **G**ifts, **L**oans, **E**xchanges **T**racking). Unfortunately, the winner was Acquire, which is *not* an acronym.

Technology

In physics, **WIMPs** are **w**eakly **i**nteractive **m**assive **p**articles. To chemists, **PEP** (**p**hospho-

enol**p**yruvate) is "an unusually energetic molecule," according to Dr. Robert Goodman, a biochemist. And **s**odium **d**odecyl **s**ulfate is abbreviated **SDS** and pronounced "suds"—most appropriate, as it is a main ingredient of shampoo.

MIRACLE is **M**ultidisciplinary **I**ntegrated **R**esearch **A**ctivities in **C**omplex **L**aboratory **E**nvironments, a project of the National Science Foundation.

In telecommunications, **p**lain **o**ld **t**elephone **s**ervice is **POTS**. It was probably inevitable that someone would dream up **PANS**, for **p**otentially **a**ttractive **n**ew **s**ervices. (In the Bronx, New York, a homeless shelter called **P**art **o**f **t**he **S**olution also houses a social action group with the name **P**eople **A**re **N**ot **S**atisfied.)

In meteorology and oceanography:

WIND, **W**eather **I**nformation **N**etwork and **D**isplay

SLOSH, **S**ea, **L**ake, **O**verland **S**urge from **H**urricanes

SPLASH, **S**pecial **P**rogram to **L**ist **A**mplitude of **S**urges from **H**urricanes

SWAMI, **S**tanford **W**orldwide **A**cquisition of **M**eteorological **I**nformation (one hopes it possesses mystical forecasting powers)

NOMAD, **N**avy **O**ceanographic **M**eteorological **A**utomatic **D**evice, the world's first nuclear-powered weather station

FAMOUS, **F**rench-**A**merican **M**id-**O**cean **U**nder-sea **S**tudy, a survey of a rift extending from the Arctic to Antarctica

SOLARIS, **S**ubmerged **O**bject **L**ocating **a**nd **R**e-trieving **I**dentification **S**ystem

HUGO, **H**ighly **U**nusual **G**eophysical **O**perations, a meteorological research vehicle unrelated to the major hurricane

SPACE, **S**atellite **P**recipitation **a**nd **C**loud **E**xperi-ment, of the **N**ational **O**ceanic and **A**tmo-spheric **A**dministration (**NOAA,** itself an acro-nym, pronounced "Noah")

JOULE is **J**oint **O**pportunities for **U**nconven-tional or **L**ong-term **E**nergy Supply. (In physics, a *joule* is a unit of energy.) **SAFARI** is the **S**outh **A**fri-can **F**undamental **A**tomic **R**eactor **I**nstallation. (**SAAFARI** is also **S**outh **A**frican **A**irways' **F**ully **A**u-tomatic **R**eservations **I**nstallation system.)

In transportation, **TRAIN** is the **T**ele-**R**ail **A**uto-mated **I**nformation **N**etwork, of the Association of American Railroads, and **DASH** is **D**owntown **A**rea **S**hort **H**ops, a bus service in Long Beach, Calif.

Corporate Acronyms: Serious Business

Company names move in cycles and fads.

In the 1970s and 1980s, an era of acquisition and diversification, huge conglomerates subsumed many types of businesses. So corporations favored initials and acronyms rather than descriptive names. US Steel became **USX**, borrowing the **X** from its stock ticker symbol (an unusual occurrence, as the ticker symbol usually comes from the company name, not the other way around).

Initials (**GE**, **ASG**, **MBPXL**) and acronyms (**NYNEX**, **UNUM**, **Alcan**, **Amstar**) inspired a wave of criticism of such names as artificial, cryptic, and "heartless." Then the trend swung back to warm and fuzzy "human" names.

Decades ago, the blend or syllabic acronym was in vogue. **SUNOCO** came from **Sun Oil Co**mpany, **SOCONY** from **S**tandard **O**il **C**ompany **o**f **N**ew **Y**ork. **ESSO** is what we call an "initialism word"—a phonetic spelling of **S.O.**, for Standard Oil Company of New Jersey. (In 1973, officials changed the name to Exxon.) **THUMS** is an acronym for what once were the five major oil companies: **T**exaco, **H**umble, **U**nion, **M**obil, and **S**hell.

Part letter acronym and part syllabic, **NECCO**, the **N**ew **E**ngland **C**onfectionery **Co**mpany, manufactures the wafer candies of the same name. The **RAND** Corporation is from **R**esearch **and** **D**evelopment.

The **Rolm** Company, a telephone equipment manufacturer (once owned by IBM and now a division of Siemens), was named in 1968 from the initials of the surnames of its founders, all electrical engineers: Gene **R**icheson, M. Kenneth **O**shman, Walter **L**owenstern, and Robert R. **M**axfield.

Invention, **D**esign, **E**ngineering **A**ssociates has an **IDEA**, which is also its stock ticker symbol.

In 1992, an ad agency established a division to advise Hollywood filmmakers, calling it **I**ntegrated **M**arketing and **A**dvertising **G**roup for **E**ntertainment, or **IMAGE**.

Fast-food chains include **Arby's**, from **R.B.** (**r**oast **b**eef), an "initialism word." **I**nternational **H**ouse **o**f **P**ancakes is **I HOP**, an abbreviation the company once disliked but now exploits in its advertising.

Overseas marketers also like acronyms. Among the airlines:

QANTAS, the Australian airline known for its cuddly koala mascot, derives from **Q**ueensland **a**nd **N**orthern **T**erritory **A**erial **S**ervices

SABENA, from *Société Anonyme Belge d'Exploitation de la Navigation Aérienne,* is the Belgian international airline

VIASA is *Venezolana Internacional de Aviación Sociedad Anónima*

An "anonymous society," contained in the two previous examples, is equivalent to our corporation or to a British limited company.

Acronymic automobile manufacturers include:

Fiat, from *Fabbrica Italiana Automobili Torino*

SAAB, from *Svenska Aeroplan Aktiebolaget* ("Swedish Airplane Company")

Simca, from ***S****ociété* ***I****ndustrielle de* ***M****écanique et de* ***Ca****rosserie* ("Mechanics and Bodywork Company"); the car is no longer manufactured

The now-departed American car called the **Reo** was named for company founder **R**ansom **E**dward **O**lds, who also gave his name to the Oldsmobile.

An around-the-world roundup of acronymic company names must also mention:

Toshiba, from **To**kyo **Shiba**ura Electric Co.

Lego, the Danish toy company, from the words ***le****g* ***go****dt* ("play well").

IKEA, the furniture chain, from the initials of founder **I**ngvar **K**amprad, and **E**lmtaryd, his family's farm in the village of **A**gunnaryd.

Agfa, the photographic film company, is from ***A****ktiengesellschaft* ***f****ür* ***A****nilinfabrikation* ("limited company for dye manufacture"). Though founded in 1867, the company did not use the acronym until 1873. As a result of a 1964 merger, the company is now Agfa-Gevaert.

Smaller businesses often display a sense of humor in their choice of names: **NYMPH** is **N**ew **Y**ork **M**aster **P**ractitioners of **H**air. **T.H.O.S.E.** cookies (**T**he **H**ouse **o**f **S**ensuous **E**ats) was founded by two women entrepreneurs in Washington, D.C. And an express freight service is called **G**uaranteed **O**ver-night **D**elivery. Its huge tractor-trailer trucks bear the enormous (and irreverent?) letters **G.O.D.**

Corporate motivational programs must have memorable names. **TEAM** (**T**eamwork, **E**ffort, **A**ttitude, **M**anage) was created by Roger Penske, head of Detroit Diesel. **STAUNCH** (**S**tress **t**hose **A**ctions **U**rgently **N**eeded to **C**heck **H**emorrhaging) was an austerity program at Advanced Micro Devices during the recession of the mid-1980s.

Marketers in search of catchy product names and slogans sometimes turn to acronyms and initialisms. Purina's successful premium pet food line is called **O.N.E.**, for **O**ptimum **N**utritional **E**ffectiveness. Anyone over the age of a baby boomer will remember **L.S./M.F.T.** (**L**ucky **S**trike **M**eans **F**ine **T**obacco).

Among the more apt acronymic titles for trade magazines:

CARS reports on ***C****ellular,* ***A****ntenna,* ***R****adar &* ***S****ecurity.*

PIERS is the ***P****ort* ***I****mport/****E****xport* ***R****eporting* ***S****ervice.*

AHAB is the ***A****ustralian* ***H****istorical* ***A****ssociation* ***B****ulletin.*

STAR is ***S****cientific and* ***T****echnical* ***A****erospace* ***R****eports.*

DATA*, The* ***D****igest of* ***A****ddiction* ***T****heory and* ***A****pplication,* is published by Brown University.

Ah Ha! is the quarterly newsletter of the **A**merican **H**olistic **H**ealth **A**ssociation.

T.W.I.C.E. (periods are their preferred style) reports on *This **W**eek **i**n **C**onsumer **E**lectronics*. In the fall of 1991, however, the publisher changed the frequency from weekly to twenty-eight issues a year, so the title is now a misnomer. (Perhaps it should be redefined as ***T**wo **W**eeks **i**n **C**onsumer **E**lectronics*.)

***T.H.E.** Journal* covers "**T**echnical **H**orizons in **E**ducation," the use of computers in teaching.

Mark the following trade shows on your calendar: A Rhode Island college sponsors the **C**ulinary **A**rts and **F**ood **E**xposition, or **CAFE**. The **S**hooting, **H**unting, **O**utdoor **T**rade show, an annual gathering in the firearms industry, is known as the **SHOT** show. And the **M**en's **A**pparel **G**uild **i**n **C**alifornia sponsors the **MAGIC** show.

A trade association of radar detector manufacturers and owners is called **R**adio **A**ssociation **D**efending **A**irwave **R**ights, which spells **RADAR**, which is already an acronym!

Of course, an acronym can be proprietary if it's registered as a trademark. But one such case is surprising. **AHANA**, meaning people of **A**frican American, **H**ispanic, **A**sian, or **N**ative **A**merican descent, was coined by two Boston College students in 1979. The school, which uses the term for a minority student program, obtained a "service mark" for the term from the U.S. Patent and Trademark Office, and insists that anyone wishing to use it must obtain the school's permission.

The **W**ashington **P**ublic **P**ower **S**upply **S**ystem, or **W.P.P.S.S.**, was popularly known as **WHOOPS**, a pseudo-acronym from its initials. This sobriquet became uncannily prophetic in 1983, when its plan to construct five nuclear plants generated huge cost overruns, leading to the biggest municipal securities default ($2.25 billion) in U.S. history.

The Financial World

WHOOPS was a disaster for bond investors, which leads us to Wall Street. That's where, in the 1980s, **V.I.P.**s masterminded **L.B.O.**s using **O.P.M.**!

Packages of securities are often given acronymic names, such as **P**erformance **E**quity **R**edemption **C**umulative **S**tock (**PERCS**), **S**hort-**T**erm **A**uction-**R**ate **S**tock (**STARS**), **S**eparate **T**rading of **R**egistered **I**nterest and **P**rincipal of **S**ecurities (**STRIPS**), **C**ertificates for **A**utomobile **R**eceivables (**CAR**s), and many others.

PORTAL is **P**rivate **O**fferings, **R**esales and **T**rading through **A**utomated **L**inkages, **BONUS** is **Bo**rrower's **O**ption for **N**otes and **U**nderwritten **S**tandby, and **ASPIRIN** (a fudged acronym) is **A**ustralian **S**tock **P**rice **R**iskless **I**ndexed **N**otes.

Packages of zero-coupon bonds sometimes bear zoological names—for example, Merrill Lynch's **LYON**s (**L**iquid-**Y**ield **O**ption **N**otes) and **TIGR**

(**T**reasury **I**nvestment **G**rowth **R**eceipts), and Salomon Brothers' **CATS** (**C**ertificates of **A**ccrual on **T**reasury **S**ecurities).

An updated children's verse might go: "Lyons and tigrs and cats . . . oh, my!" You'll also find:

COLTS, **C**ontinuously **O**ffered **L**ong-**T**erm **S**ecurities

COUGARS, **C**ertificates **o**n **G**overnment **R**eceipts (an imperfect acronym)

OPOSSMS, **O**ptions to **P**urchase **o**r **S**ell **S**pecific **M**ortgage-backed **S**ecurities

SPDRs (pronounced "spiders"), **S**tandard & **P**oor's (500 stock index) **D**epository **R**eceipts

Such repackaged bonds are generically called "felines" and "animals." (One day, perhaps a broker will announce the **B**asket **o**f **W**orld-**W**ide **O**ptions on **W**arrants, or **BOWWOW**!)

Unfortunately, many security names fall into the "pseudo-acronym" category we discussed earlier. The **F**ederal **N**ational **M**ortgage **A**ssociation, **F.N.M.A.**, and the bonds it sells, are universally known as Fannie Mae. This formula is echoed by the **G**overnment **N**ational **M**ortgage **A**ssociation, **G.N.M.A.**, or Ginnie Mae. The mortgaged-backed securities of the **R**esolution **T**rust **C**orporation, **R.T.C.**, are Ritzie Mae. Some states have picked up on the pattern. Bonds of the **S**tate **o**f **N**ew **Y**ork

Mortgage **A**gency, **S.N.M.A.**, or **SONYMA**, are Sonny Mae.

CHIPS is the **C**learing **H**ouse **I**nterbank **P**ayment **S**ystem. Its British counterpart is the **C**learing **H**ouse **A**utomated **P**ayments **S**ystem, or (appropriately enough) **CHAPS**. **SWIFT** is the **S**ociety for **W**orldwide **I**nterbank **F**inancial **T**elecommunications. **BIDS** was the **B**ritish **I**nstitute of **D**ealers in **S**ecurities (now defunct).

In the accounting, taxation, pension planning, and insurance professions, acronyms, some better than others, proliferate. A small sampling:

An **E**mployee **S**tock **O**wnership **P**lan is an **ESOP** (pronounced like the fabler). **TEFRA** was the **T**ax **E**quity and **F**iscal **R**esponsibility **A**ct. The 1986 **C**onsolidated **O**mnibus **B**udget **R**econciliation **A**ct is **COBRA**. A **Q**ualified **T**erminable **I**nterest **P**roperty is a **Q-TIP**. The **F**inancial **A**ccounting **S**tandards **B**oard, **F.A.S.B.**, which sets rules for the profession, is known to all concerned by the pseudoacronym "fazz-bee." **FIFO** and **LIFO** are inventory accounting terms meaning **f**irst **i**n, **f**irst **o**ut, and **l**ast **i**n, **f**irst **o**ut.

The banking industry is rife with acronyms, from **IRA**s to **PIN**s. One bank's loan program is called **F**inancial **O**ptions for **C**ollege and **U**niversity **S**tudents, or **FOCUS**. The **N**ew **Y**ork **C**ash **E**xchange, a network of automatic teller machines, inspired some of its members to advertise "We're a **NYCE** Bank."

Bank examiners employ a variety of rating systems to measure the health of an institution. One is called **CAMEL**, for **c**apital, **a**sset quality, **m**anagement, **e**arnings, and **l**iquidity.

In a marketing incentive program launched in 1992, a group of retailers agreed to fund an annuity policy for customers, with contributions based on purchases. It's temptingly titled **START** ("**S**pend **T**oday **a**nd **R**etire **T**omorrow").

Federal and Local Government

Bureaucracy is, of course, a fertile source of initialisms and acronyms. Here is a sampling of the most interesting:

REAP, the **R**ural **E**nvironmental **A**ssistance **P**rogram of the U.S. Department of Agriculture.

SWEAT, **S**tudent **W**ork **E**xperience **a**nd **T**raining, a federally funded summer jobs program preparing young people for careers in mental health institutions.

PASSIM, the **P**resident's **A**dvisory **S**taff on **S**cientific **I**nformation **M**anagement. (*Passim* is Latin for "in various places," leading one to wonder how members are assembled for meetings.)

SPEED, **S**cheduled **P**rocurement of **E**ssential **E**quipment **D**eliveries, a Postal Service program. (We shall refrain from comment.)

OCWA, **O**nondaga **C**ounty (New York) **W**ater **A**uthority, is pronounced as a homophone of *aqua*.

FACE IT, the **F**oreign **A**gents **C**ompulsory **E**thics **i**n **T**rade Act, is clever, but spoiled by the absence of the final word.

Although a 1987 Filipino rebel operation didn't achieve its goal, it deserves an award for acronymic dexterity: **R**emove **A**quino from **M**alacañang (Palace) **B**efore **O**ctober, or **RAMBO**.

SWAT, for **S**pecial **W**eapons **a**nd **T**actics, is a familiar police acronym. Here are a few more:

FIST, **F**ugitive **I**nvestigative **S**trike **T**eam, a joint federal-local program

STRIDE, **S**ystem **t**o **R**etrieve **I**nformation from **D**rug **E**vidence

PATROL, **P**rogram for **A**dministrative **T**raffic **R**eports **O**n-**L**ine

CLEAT, **C**ombined **L**aw **E**nforcement **A**ssociations of **T**exas

SEARCH, **S**ystem for **E**lectronic **A**nalysis and **R**etrieval of **C**riminal **H**istories, a U.S. Department of Justice program that was succeeded by the National Crime Information Center

CULTURE, **C**reative **U**se of **L**eisure **T**ime **U**nder **R**estrictive **E**nvironments, a prison program

A sophisticated $250,000 device, equipped with weapons and a video camera, was designed to aid military and police personnel in potentially violent confrontations. Its name? **P**rogrammable **R**obot **O**bserver **W**ith **L**ogical **E**nemy **R**esponse, or **PROWLER**. It's manufactured by Robot Defense Systems, Thornton, Colo.

RICO, for **R**acketeer **I**nfluenced and **C**orrupt **O**rganizations Act, is a 1970 federal anticrime law that is often criticized for its harsh penalties and use in civil cases. The name was created by G. Robert Blakey, a professor at Notre Dame Law School, who helped draft the legislation.

Some say the expansion is cumbersome, and indeed it is often rendered incorrectly. It's frequently contended that RICO intentionally echoes the nickname of Caesar Enrico Bandello, the gangster portrayed by Edward G. Robinson in the 1930 movie *Little Caesar.* Professor Blakey, although an admitted film enthusiast, is coy on this point.

The FBI's **COINTELPRO**, one of many espionage acronyms, comes from **Co**unter**intel**ligence **Pro**gram. Between 1956 and 1971, the program roused controversy for its questionable techniques directed against, among others, groups opposed to the war in Vietnam.

Some anticrime citizens' groups:

FORCE, **F**riends **O**rganizing to **R**educe **C**rime **E**verywhere

STRESS, **St**op the **R**obberies, **E**njoy **S**afe **S**treets, a Detroit program that's now defunct

SHARE, **S**urvivors of **H**omicide **a**nd **R**elated **E**ffects

C.H.U.C.K., the **C**ommittee to **H**alt **U**seless **C**ollege **K**illings, opposes dangerous fraternity initiation ceremonies and hazings. Founded by a Long Island, N.Y., woman whose son died in a hazing incident, the group's acronym memorializes his name.

Political Acronymy

Some acronyms memorably capture the spirit of American politics.

During World War II, Representative Karl E. Mundt created the facetious **G**uild of **W**ashington **I**ncompetent **B**ureaucratic **I**dea **T**hroatcutters, or **GWIBIT**. A "gwibitizer," explained the congressman, actively sabotages progress, in contrast to the kibitzer, who merely observes.

A **MEGO**, from "**m**y **e**yes **g**laze **o**ver," describes boring and soporific issues and policies.

Pompous, platitudinous, pious political prose. That's the meaning of **BOMFOG**, from "the **B**rotherhood **o**f **M**an under the **F**atherhood **o**f **G**od." The phrase was used, seriously, by Nelson Rockefeller in the 1964 presidential campaign; Nelson in turn had borrowed the overblown locution from his father,

John D. Rockefeller II. Reporters seized on the acronym and used it disparagingly.

If you're planning to run for Congress, please don't confuse BOMFOG with **BOGSTAT**. In 1986, Congressman Les Aspin characterized the Reagan administration's formulation of foreign policy as "a **b**unch **o**f **g**uys **s**itting **t**alking **a**round a **t**able," hence BOGSTAT. The acronym is sometimes rendered as **BOGSAT**—which seems to suggest an unlikely scene of silence.

In his 1903 book *The Varieties of Religious Experience,* philosopher-psychologist William James sounded a clarion call for the "moral equivalent of war." He visualized a peaceful crusade that would galvanize the emotions and will of humanity as powerfully as bellicose activities have done throughout history. Seven years later, his optimistic sentiment, which was characteristic of late-nineteenth-century England, was repeated and heavily publicized in magazine articles and in pamphlets distributed by peace groups. One such brochure took the phrase as its title.

In 1977, Jimmy Carter invoked James's inspiring message in a major national speech, declaring the **mo**ral **e**quivalent **o**f **w**ar against a then-worrisome "energy crisis." Unfortunately for the President, *New York Times* humor columnist Russell Baker mocked Carter's words as a plaintive "**MEOW!**" The acronym, noted Baker about the challenge, "makes it sound like a pussy-cat affair."

During the 1992 election campaigns, two groups

were busy raising money for pro-choice female candidates. The Democratic side has **Emily**'s List but no Emily; the name is an acronym for **E**arly **m**oney **i**s **l**ike **y**east. ("It makes the dough rise," they pun.) Meanwhile, pro-choice Republican candidates have a **Wish** List, for **W**omen **i**n the **S**enate and **H**ouse.

The late science-fiction writer Robert Heinlein coined the libertarian rallying cry **TANSTAAFL** for **T**here **A**in't **N**o **S**uch **T**hing **as a** **F**ree **L**unch! In Heinlein's 1966 novel *The Moon Is a Harsh Mistress,* a character explains: "One way or other, what you get, you pay for." "Free lunches"—but only with the purchase of a drink—were offered by nineteenth-century tavern keepers. The phrase and the acronym are sometimes erroneously credited to economist Milton Friedman, who in his books and *Newsweek* columns did help give the expression wide currency.

Military and Space

The armed forces are skilled at recruiting initialisms, acronyms, and abbreviations into their ranks.

"The military seems particularly afflicted by an acute case of acronymitis," noted *The New York Times* in a 1991 dispatch from Saudi Arabia. News coverage of the Persian Gulf War brought a host of abbreviations, new and old, to public attention.

The British derogated journalists, politicians, and noncombat officers as **PONTS** (**p**eople **o**f **n**o **t**actical **s**ignificance) or **PONSI** (**p**erson **o**f **n**o **s**trategic **i**mportance).

Perhaps the most widely reported abbreviation from the Mideast conflict was the initialism **M.R.E.**s, meaning **m**eals **r**eady to **e**at. The vacuum-packed field rations were cynically redefined by soldiers as "**m**eals **r**ejected by **E**thiopians."

From **K.P.** to the **DEW** line, many military abbreviations have become part of the language of civilians. (The origins of the militarily coined words **snafu**, **Jeep**, and **seabee**, which entered civilian English, were discussed in Chapter 4.) In the 1949 film *I Was a Male War Bride,* Cary Grant is befuddled by a succession of doors that display cryptic military initialisms.

In World War I, **A.W.O.L.** was an initialism, and in World War II it became the acronym **AWOL.** The term dates at least to 1919, although some word sleuths trace it as far back as the Civil War and the early nineteenth century.

For acronymic purposes, **OHIO** is not a state but "**O**ver the **H**ill **i**n **O**ctober!," a popular slogan and graffito of draftees in 1941. The conscription law passed in 1940 required just one year of service, and October was the month the guys thought they could go home. Of course, the Pearl Harbor attack on December 7 changed everyone's plans.

G.I. as a name for an Army soldier appears to date from about 1935. It is usually acknowledged to derive from **g**overnment (or **g**eneral) **i**ssue clothing and equipment enlisted personnel receive. Some propose another origin: the **g**alvanized **i**ron trash can. Eminent slang lexicographer Eric Partridge emphatically disputed this suggested etymology. As an adjective, it is applied to almost everything (often pejoratively), from "G.I. haircut" to "G.I. blues" to "the G.I. way."

A particularly intriguing illustration of acronymia is the Navy's **SEAL** unit, derived from **Se**a-**A**ir-**L**and. Members are called SEALs, which communicates a suitably aquatic image.

The **Enola Gay**, the name of the plane that dropped the first atomic bomb, is sometimes said to have been coined from the phrase "**Y**ou **a**re **g**oing **alone.**" The first three words allegedly became a "backward acronym," and the final word was simply reversed. It's just another myth. Enola Gay was the name of the mother of the pilot, Colonel Paul Tibbets.

The Navy is partial to the syllabic acronym. For example, **COMNAVAIR** stands for **Com**mander, **Nav**al **Air** Force. Sometimes this gets a bit out of hand. Consider the twenty-five-letter example **COMCRUDESLANTSUPPGRUNORVA**, for **Com**mander, **Cru**iser-**Des**troyer Forces, At**lant**ic **Supp**ort **Gr**o**u**p, **Nor**folk, **V**irgini**a.**

As noted in Chapter 3, World War II considerably increased the supply of military acronyms.

When females became eligible for military service, acronymic designations for the new units were devised. **WAC**s are members of the **W**omen's **A**rmy **C**orps (founded in 1942 as **WAAC,** for **W**omen's

Army **A**uxiliary **C**orps). The Navy has its **W**omen **A**ccepted for **V**olunteer **E**mergency **S**ervice or **WAVES**, created in 1942. The appropriately nautical-sounding acronym survives, although the expansion is obsolete. **WAF**s are **W**omen in the **A**ir **F**orce (1940; originally **WAFS**—Women's **A**uxiliary **F**errying **S**quadron).

The formula changed for women members of the Coast Guard Reserve, who are called **SPAR**s, a loan from the Guard's slogan ***S**emper **Par**atus* ("Always Ready").

Britain and Australia formed similar units. The United Kingdom's **W**omen's **R**oyal **N**aval **S**ervice (1917; reactivated 1939), W.R.N.S., became, via the interpolation of a letter, **WRENS**—a pun on "bird," a British colloquialism for an attractive female.

During both world wars, the members of another British branch, the **F**irst **A**id **N**ursing **Y**eomanry, were known as **FANY**s or Fannies. But the "fanny" double entendre requires some explanation.

Notes British lexicographer Gyles Brandreth: "Though it is most commonly used as a euphemism for 'buttocks,' it can also refer [in the United Kingdom] to the female genitals." Although now archaic, this latter sense was the one that was prevalent in England during the war years. The sexual meaning of fanny predated the U.S. sense by seventy or more years.

Long gone from the ranks of both nations are the **WIRES** (**W**omen **i**n **R**adio and **E**lectrical **S**ervice), along with the **WINS**, **WIPS**, **WOWS**, and **WASPS**.

Military weaponry armed with acronymic names includes **MIRV**, for **m**ultiple **i**ndependently target-able **r**eentry **v**ehicles (the Army speaks of "mirving" a bomber, a functional shift to a verb). The Pentagon also has these evocative armaments:

HAWK, **h**oming **a**ll the **w**ay **k**iller

SLAM, **s**upersonic **l**ow-**a**ltitude **m**issile

HARM, **h**igh-**a**cceleration **r**ocket-**m**issile

DASH, **d**rone **a**nti-**s**ubmarine **h**elicopter

AMMO, **A**rmy **m**obile **m**issile **o**peration

SWARMS, **s**mall **w**arhead **a**nd **r**eentry **m**ultiple **s**ystem

RESCU, **r**ocket-**e**jection **s**eat **c**atapult **u**pward

EGADS, **e**lectronic **g**round **a**utomatic **d**estruct **s**equencer—the signal given to destroy a missile in flight

Egads! No wonder there's a **W**orldwide **A**mmunition **R**eporting **S**ystem (**WARS**)!

The nuclear defense policy of **M**utual **A**ssured **D**estruction, or **MAD**, governed U.S. foreign policy for decades. Some considered it an ironically apposite acronym. In 1964, then Secretary of Defense Robert McNamara coined the phrase "assured destruction." Donald Brennan, a defense analyst at the Hudson Institute (and a critic of the policy), added the "mutual" in 1969. More optimistically if less meaningfully, Max Kampelman coined **M**utual **A**ssured **S**urvival, or **MAS**, in 1985.

The nuclear threat led to years of disarmament negotiations between the United States and what was then the U.S.S.R.

State Department officer Robert Martin coined **SALT** (**S**trategic **A**rms **L**imitation **T**alks) in 1969. Eugene Rostow, adviser to President Johnson, takes the credit for **START** (**St**rategic **A**rms **R**eduction **T**alks).

In 1989, yet another round of negotiations, this time in Vienna, was originally named **C**onventional **A**rmed **F**orces in **E**urope, or **CAFE**. The media began using the acronym. Then delegates apparently decided that it sounded too frivolous and dropped the "Armed." Thus did a potentially tasty acronym become an unappetizing initialism.

At *The Economist,* the highly regarded newsweekly, disappointed editors, tongues firmly planted in cheeks, suggested some alternative names: "**S**imultaneous **A**rms **C**utting and **H**armonization in the **E**uropean **R**egion" and "**T**alks **o**n **R**eductions of **T**roops in **E**urope," which together spell **SACHER TORTE**.

The **S**trategic **D**efense **I**nitiative program was never comfortable either as **S.D.I.** or with its "Star Wars" nickname. In 1985, William Safire, in his *New York Times Magazine* language column, issued a call for a new acronym. Six hundred readers responded. Among the cleverest entries: **SANE**

(**S**ecurity **A**gainst **N**uclear **E**xtinction) and **AEGIS** (**A**merican **E**arth **G**uard **i**n **S**pace).

More military coinages:

BASH, **b**ird **a**ircraft **s**trike **h**azard

ALOFT, **a**irborne **l**ight **o**ptical **f**iber **t**echnology

BIRDIE, **b**attery **i**ntegration and **r**adar **di**splay **e**quipment

CHASE, **c**ut **h**oles **a**nd **s**ink '**e**m, a sophisticated Navy technique for disposing of old boats

SCAN, **s**elf-**c**orrecting **a**utomatic **n**avigator

AUDIT, **A**ircraft **U**nitized **D**iagnostic **I**nspection and **T**est

SUDS, **S**ilhouetting **U**nderwater **D**etecting **S**ystem, for submarines

AGREE, **A**dvisory **G**roup on **R**eliability of **E**lectronic **E**quipment

DIPOLES, **D**efense **I**ntelligence **P**hotoreconnaissance **O**n-**L**ine **E**xploitation **S**ystem

CHAMPION, **C**ompatible **H**ardware **a**nd **Mi**lestone **P**rogram for **I**ntegrating **O**rganizational **N**eeds

MOOT means **M**ove **O**ut **o**f **T**own, the reduction of troop concentrations in cities. **MOOSE** was **M**ove **O**ut **o**f **S**aigon **E**xpeditiously.

Inspirational military acronyms include **CAN DO** (**C**onsolidated **A**ccelerated **N**avy **D**ocumentation **O**rganization) and the Army's **MASTER KEY** (**Ma**nagership of **S**oldier **T**raining, **E**ducation and **R**eadiness with **K**nowledge and **E**xcellence **Y**ear-round).

When I was in the Navy, stationed at Clark Air Base in the Philippines, many service people purchased tacky ceramic sculptures of elephants and shipped them home. Enlisted postal clerks became so tired of handling the crates that they unkindly dubbed the pachyderms **BUFE**s (pronounced "BOO-fees"), meaning **b**ig **u**gly **f**at **e**lephants. (The **F** also had an alternative meaning.) I'm told that the same phenomenon and acronym were common at American bases throughout Southeast Asia.

Space acronyms:

MOUSE, **m**inimum **o**rbital **u**nmanned **s**atellite of the **e**arth, a miniature satellite

ROOST, **r**eusable **o**ne-stage **o**rbital **s**pace **t**ruck

EMPIRE, **E**arly **M**anned **P**lanetary-**I**nterplanetary **R**ound-trip **E**xperiment

SCRAM, **s**pace **c**apsule **r**egulator **a**nd **m**onitor

SMART, **s**atellite **m**aintenance **a**nd **r**epair **t**echniques

ROCKET, **R**and's **O**mnibus **C**alculator of the **K**inetics of **E**arth **T**rajectories (**RAND** is itself an acronym, as noted earlier in this chapter)

SCHMOO, **s**pace **c**argo **h**andler and **m**anipulator for **o**rbital **o**perations (from the cartoon characters created by Al Capp)

Earlier, we talked about **U.F.O.**s. We earthlings are ready for extraterrestrial encounters—acronymically, at least:

SETI is the **S**earch for **E**xtra**t**errestrial **I**ntelligence, a federal project

SAUCERS is the **S**pace **a**nd **U**nexplained **C**elestial **E**vents **R**esearch **S**ociety

SPLAASH is the **S**pacecraft **P**rotective **L**anding **A**rea for the **A**dvancement of **S**cience and **Hu**manities, near Mount Rainier, Wash.

PROTEUS is the **P**roject to **R**esearch **O**bjects, **T**heories, **E**xtraterrestrials and **U**nusual **S**ightings (Proteus was a mythological sea god who could assume many forms)

Film and Television Acronyms

Here is a T.V. and movie guide you won't find in your Sunday newspaper. It will enable you to plan a schedule of exclusively acronymic entertainment. But heed well this caveat: An acronymic title is not necessarily a guarantee of quality!

We shall ignore titles that are merely initialistic, such as ***S.O.B.*** (1981) and ***D.O.A.*** (1949 and 1988), in order to focus on pure acronyms. Of course, no one is expected to sound out each letter, so periods are superfluous. But some producers evidently think they need to telegraph their cleverness. We shall reproduce their punctuation.

D.A.R.Y.L., **D**ata **A**nalyzing **R**obot **Y**outh **L**ifeform, is an android tyke in a so-so 1985 science-fiction movie.

C.H.U.D., **C**annibalistic **H**umanoid **U**nderground **D**wellers, was a 1984 horror film. The surprise ending, which I shall resist the temptation to reveal, turned on an alternative expansion (the "real" meaning) of the acronym. A sequel followed—or is that redundant? (For a while, *chud* was college slang for a gross person.)

C.H.O.M.P.S., a 1979 domestic comedy, features an inventor who builds a bionic dog to scare off burglars. The contrived acronym means **C**anine **Hom**e **P**rotection **S**ystem.

F.I.S.T., a 1978 drama, stars Sylvester Stallone as a union boss resembling Jimmy Hoffa. The title means **F**ederation of **I**nter-**S**tate **T**ruckers.

S*H*E is entirely unrelated to the various filmings of the classic H. Rider Haggard novel. This one is a 1980 made-for-television movie about the adventures of a female superspy, or **S**ecurities **H**azards **E**xpert. Despite a script by James Bond writer Richard Maibaum and some well-known stars, it didn't fare well.

One of the best-known Hollywood acronyms is **HAL**, the computer in *2001: A Space Odyssey.* Rumors still surface claiming that the name was created by subtracting one letter sequentially from each of the letters **I.B.M.** Pure coincidence, insists *2001* author Arthur C. Clarke. "I've been trying to put that myth to rest for the past twenty years," he told *The New York Times* in 1992. **HAL** really stands for "**h**euristically programmed **al**gorithmic computer."

The real-life Soviet spy agency **SMERSH** (see page 216) inspired Ian Fleming's fictitious **S.P.E.C.T.R.E.** (**Sp**ecial **E**xecutor for **C**ounterintelligence, **T**errorism, **R**evenge, and **E**xtortion), James Bond's nemesis in seven movies. The rights to the use of S.P.E.C.T.R.E. have been tangled in assorted lawsuits for years, which helps explain why the evil organization doesn't appear in all 007 films.

In the 1960s, acronymic secret agencies were all over the T.V. dial. *The Man from **U.N.C.L.E.*** ran from 1964 to 1968. The agency abbreviated in the title is the **U**nited **N**etwork **C**ommand for **L**aw and **E**nforcement. Sam Rolfe, one of *U.N.C.L.E.*'s creators, frankly conceded that the acronym was intended to suggest both the United Nations and Uncle Sam. The bad-guy agency **THRUSH** originally had no expansion. But in novelizations of the series, it became the **T**echnical **H**ierarchy for the **R**emoval of **U**ndesirables and the **S**ubjugation of **H**umanity.

The season following *U.N.C.L.E.*'s premiere, Mel Brooks's *Get Smart* (1965–70) appeared. Helping to spoof the spy genre were CONTROL and its rival secret agency KAOS, "which, like CONTROL, is not now and has never been an acronym," notes Donna McCrohan in *The Life and Times of Maxwell Smart,* the semi-official book about the show.

In the B.B.C. cult science-fiction series *Dr. Who* (which premiered in England in 1963 and in the United States in 1968), the vehicle that transports the doctor to any desired place or period in the universe is called the **Tardis** (**T**ime **a**nd **r**elative **d**imension **i**n **s**pace).

M*A*S*H began as a novel by Richard Hooker, followed by the film (1970) and the acclaimed television series (1972–83). The title is a genuine Korean War acronym, circa 1952, which, as millions of viewers know, means "**m**obile **A**rmy **s**urgical **h**ospital." Robert Altman, director of the film, may be partial to acronymic titles, as he also directed ***H.E.A.L.T.H.*** (**H**appiness, **E**nergy, **a**nd **L**ongevity **T**hrough **H**ealth), a far less successful 1979 satire.

More T.V. series:

CHiPs (1977–83) followed the adventures of two **C**alifornia **Hi**ghway **P**atrol cops.

S.W.A.T. (1975–77) featured the exploits of a **s**pecial **w**eapons **a**nd **t**actics unit aiding the California police. It took some flak as the most violent show on the air at the time.

*The **L**ife **a**nd **T**imes of **E**ddie **R**oberts,* also known as ***LATER*** (1980), was a sitcom guilty of selective capitalization.

***T.H.E.** Cat* (1966–67) starred Robert Loggia as a burglar-turned-bodyguard conveniently named **T**homas **H**ewitt **E**dward Cat.

Other acronymic spy agencies cropped up in series aimed at children:

The Kids from ***C.A.P.E.R.*** (1976–77) was a sitcom with four teenage crime-fighters. The somewhat forced agency name meant **C**ivilian **A**uthority for the **P**rotection of **E**veryone, **R**egardless. Genuine simian actors constituted the cast of *Lancelot Link, Secret Chimp* (1970–72). The hero worked for **A.P.E.**, the **A**gency to **P**revent **E**vil, and fought the **C**riminal **H**eadquarters for **U**nderground **M**aster **P**lan, or **C.H.U.M.P.** The **M**obile **A**rmy **S**trike **C**ommand was featured in ***M.A.S.K.*** (1985).

Although *Knight Rider* (1982–86) was not an acronym, the hero worked for **FLAG**, the **F**oundation for **L**aw **a**nd **G**overnment, and his high-tech car was named **KITT** (**K**night **I**ndustries **T**wo **T**housand).

Lest we forget, the cry "**SHAZAM!**" turned Billy Batson into Captain Marvel. The acronym represented the powers of **S**olomon, **H**ercules, **A**tlas, **Z**eus, **A**chilles, and **M**ercury. (Do you really need to know the corresponding heroines for Mary Marvel?)

More Cultural Acronymia

Let's go to the theater. A familiar acronymic word with World War II origins (see page 104) became the title of a 1944 Broadway comedy.

Snafu, by Louis Solomon and Harold Buchman, and directed by theater legend George Abbott, related the tribulations of an underage soldier when he is found out and shipped home. Reviews of the comedy ranged widely from tepid to amused, and *Snafu* ran 158 performances. A year later, Hollywood released a film version starring Robert Benchley. (In 1976, an unrelated sitcom pilot called *Snafu* didn't make it to home T.V. screens, but remains notable for casting Jay Leno as a soldier in a tiny supporting role.)

A 1966 Broadway black comedy about a mysterious organization dedicated to the altruistic goal of murdering nasty people bore the unlikely title ***UTBU***, for **U**nhealthy **T**o **B**e **U**npleasant. Heading a talented cast, Tony Randall was the intended victim, a failed actor determined to knock off his elderly mother for her cash. Critical reaction was mixed to negative, and the show ran an anemic seven performances. Fortunately for playwright James Kirkwood, nine years later he was to collaborate in the creation of a musical called *A Chorus Line*.

New York's **T**heatre **a**nd **D**ance **A**lliance, or

TADA!, stages performances for children. **T**heater **W**orks **E**merging **E**xperimental **D**irections is **T.W.E.E.D.** The **S**hubert **E**ntertainment and **A**rts **T**icketing **S**ystem, not surprisingly, sells **SEATS**.

In pop music, the **Bee Gees** name comes from **B.G.**, **B**rothers **G**ibb. **R.E.M.** is **R**apid **E**ye **M**ovement. **B.A.D.** is **B**ig **A**udio **D**ynamite. **INXS** stands for **in excess**.

KISS is sometimes identified as an acronym for "**K**nights **i**n the **S**ervice of **S**atan." But that idea is "a ridiculous and totally false rumor," according to a rock music expert I interviewed.

The Swedish group **ABBA** took its name from the initials of the first names of its four members: **A**gnetha Faltskög, **B**enny Andersson, **B**jörn Ulvaeus, and **A**nni-Frid Lyngstad. Coincidentally, Abba was also a Stockholm fish cannery. (Presumably the singers were unaware that Abba is the Aramaic and Hebrew word for "father" and was used in prayers by early Christians.)

Radio station call letters often spell out intelligible messages.

In some cases, the letters were assigned by the government, then expansions were creatively read into them. In other instances, stations requested specific letter combinations that would spell an initialistic or acronymic slogan. The following selections are from a list of seven hundred call signs, and their origins and meanings, which computer consultant Bob Nelson of Dallas compiled.

Pine Bluff, Ark., grows **KOTN**. Fairbanks, Alas.,

paddles a **KIAK**. In Carmel, Calif., **KRML** approximates the city's name.

Chicago's **WBBM** boasts "**W**e **B**roadcast **B**etter **M**usic." Rutland, Vt.'s, **WSYB** announces "**W**e **S**erve **Y**ou **B**est." Gainesville, Fla.'s, **WGGG** proudly intones "**W**atch **G**reater **G**ainesville **G**row." For its French-speaking listeners, Ottawa has the inviting **CHEZ**.

In many cases, call letters represent or suggest the station's dial locations in Roman numerals, including Beaumont, Tx.'s, **KLVI** (560 AM).

Acronymic awards include the following kudos: The **PATSY** (**P**icture [sometimes **P**erforming] **A**nimal **T**op **S**tar of the **Y**ear). The **RITA**, the Romance Writers' Association award named for cofounder Rita Clay Estrada. (It was subsequently reinterpreted as "**R**omance **I**s **T**reasured **A**lways.") The **Obie** is short for **O**ff-**B**roadway. The **Play** is the **P**rogram **L**ength **A**ward of the **Y**ear, for TV infomercials. The **AWGIE** is presented by the **A**ustralian **W**riters' **G**uild.

Toys include Mattell's **CUTIE** (**C**oolest **U**ltra **T**iny **I**ndividuals on **E**arth) and **MUSCLE** (**M**illions of **U**nusual **S**mall **C**reatures **L**urking **E**verywhere), and Milton-Bradley's **THINGS** (**T**otally **H**ilarious **I**ncredibly **N**eat **G**ames of **S**kill).

Literary Acronyms

In 1926, the English poet laureate John Masefield published a novel titled ***Odtaa***, meaning **O**ne **d**amn

thing **a**fter **a**nother. Arthur Herzog's 1983 novel about big-time corporate warfare is called ***L.S.I.T.T.***, for **L**et's **S**tick **I**t **t**o **T**hem.

Robert Thornton's tongue-in-cheek *Lexicon of **In**tentionally **A**mbiguous **R**ecommendations,* or ***LIAR*** (1988), explains how to compose an unfavorable letter of reference that protects you from retribution should your comments be disclosed. (To describe someone who rarely appears for work: "A man like him is hard to find.")

Ken Kesey's 1992 novel *Sailor Song,* set in Alaska in the future, features the **L**oyal **O**rder of the **U**nder**d**ogs (**LOUD**) and **D**escendants of **E**arly **A**boriginal **P**eoples (**DEAP**s).

Thomas Pynchon, whose novels are set in a pessimistic and paranoid world oppressed by technology and bureaucracy, frequently employs initialisms and acronyms for satirical effect. His best-known work, *Gravity's Rainbow* (1973), is an apocalyptic fantasy containing **P**sychological **I**ntelligence **Sc**hemes for **E**xpediting **S**urrender (**PISCES**) and the **A**llied **C**learing **H**ouse, **T**echnical **U**nits, **N**orthern **G**ermany (**ACHTUNG**).

Several science-fiction writers love to play with acronyms.

Keith Laumer's 1962 short story "Cultural Exchange" (reprinted in his 1978 book *Retief at Large*) features the squabbling bureaucratic agencies **MUDDLE** (**M**anpower **U**tilization **D**irectorate, **D**ivision of **L**ibraries and **E**ducation) and **MEDDLE** (**M**otorized **E**quipment **D**epot, **D**ivision of **L**oans and **E**xchanges). Larry Niven created **ARM**, for **A**malgamated **R**egional **M**ilitia, a U.N. police force of the future. "The acronym came first," he admits. "I had to make up words and background to fit the initials." For a famous acronym coined by science-fiction legend Robert Heinlein, turn back to page 172. (To boldly go on a journey into the language of science fiction, acronymic and otherwise, see Roberta Rogow's fascinating book *Futurespeak.*)

Coinages From Classics and Mythology

A fertile source of acronymic nomenclature is the ancient world. It's so popular, in fact, that numerous alternative expansions exist for each name. We'll limit ourselves to one specimen for each famous personage. Consider first these three philosophical examples:

ARISTOTLE, **A**nnual **R**eview and **I**nformation **S**ymposium on the **T**echnology **o**f **T**raining, **L**earning and **E**ducation, a Department of Defense program

SOCRATES, **S**ystem for **O**rganizing **C**ontent to **R**eview **a**nd **T**each **E**ducational **S**ubjects

PLATO, **P**rogrammed **L**ogic for **A**utomatic **T**eaching **O**perations, a computer language created at the University of Illinois

And these from mythology, tragedy, and reality:

ICARUS, **I**nter**c**ontinental **A**erospacecraft **R**ange **U**nlimited **S**ystem

ATLAS, **A**dvanced **T**actical **L**ightweight **A**vionics **S**ystem

MIDAS, **M**odified **I**ntegration **D**igital **A**nalog **S**imulator

HERCULES, **H**igh-**E**nergy **R**adiation **C**amera **U**sing **L**ight-**E**mitting **S**howers

APOLLO, **A**rticle **P**rocurement with **O**n-**L**ine **L**ocal **O**rdering

MINERVA, **M**ultiple **I**nput **N**etwork for **E**valuating **R**eactions, **V**otes, and **A**ttitudes, a British survey tool

CAESAR, **C**omputerized **A**utomation by **E**lectronic **S**ystem with **A**utomated **R**eservation

CASSANDRA, **C**hromatogram **A**utomatic **S**oaking **S**canning **an**d **D**igital **R**ecording **A**pparatus

OEDIPUS, **O**xford **E**nglish **D**ictionary **I**nputting, **P**roofing, and **U**pdating **S**ervice

Infelicitous Acronymy

We have examined numerous examples of acronyms that possess varying degrees of relevance. Now it must be noted once again that certain acronyms are less than apropos. In fact, they can sometimes be downright inappropriate, irrelevant, incongruous, or pejorative. Not to mention amusing.

For example, in 1983, when Eastman Kodak realized that its new **U.S**. **E**quipment **D**ivision formed the acronym **USED**, executives quickly renamed it.

Is the **E**astern **V**erbal **I**nvestigators **L**eague really **EVIL**? Is the **B**eryllium **O**xide **R**eactor **E**xperiment a **BORE**?

Does it inspire confidence among environmentalists that an **o**ffshore **o**il **p**ollution **s**leeve spells **OOPS**? Ditto for the **O**rganization of **O**il **P**roducing **S**tates and the **O**ffice for **O**perations in **P**olitical **S**ystems. The computer industry has **o**bject-**o**riented **p**rogramming **s**ystems, and a Manhattan furniture store is called **O**riginals **o**n **P**ermanent **S**ale.

Washington, D.C., is no stranger to this phenomenon. William Safire notes that the **L**aw **o**f the **S**ea **T**reaty spells **LOST**, an "unfortunate acronym." But he admits that as a Nixon administration staffer in 1971, he created the name **C**ommittee to **Re-E**lect the **P**resident—oblivious to the acronym **CREEP**, which was first spotted by Robert Dole. Of course, the coinage was destined for infamy in the wake of the Watergate scandal.

The **D**epartment of **U**rban **D**evelopment wisely changed its name to Department of Housing and Urban Development. And we almost had a **D**epartment of **I**ndustrial and **E**conomic **D**evelopment.

In 1947, Congress created an agency it christened the **N**ational **M**ilitary **E**stablishment. After a staffer pointed out the possible misinterpretation that could be generated by the initials **N.M.E.**, the name was quickly dropped. But it took till 1949 to come up with Department of Defense. ("N.M.E." was an intentional letter pun more than a century before, and it continues to be reinvented, as witness the pop group **N**ew **M**usical **E**xpress.)

In 1952, **Sec**retary of **Def**ense Robert A. Lovett told an audience that he preferred his title to be abbreviated **secdef**, a syllabic acronym, rather than **S.O.D.**, the initialism. His tongue-in-cheek explanation alluded to a possible confusion with "S.O.B." But he omitted mention of another meaning of *sod*—especially in England.

In 1984, the Reagan administration proposed a **Y**outh **E**mployment **O**pportunity **W**age, or **YEOW**! Supporters of the bill were not disconcerted by the loud acronym.

The military also displays a talent for odd choices. The Navy title **C**ommander**-in-C**hief, **U.S.** (Fleet), or **CINCUS**, proved to be an unintentional homophone for "sink us." It was changed after the Pearl Harbor bombing to **COMINCH** (**Com**mander-**in-Ch**ief).

Among other strange military choices:

DUMB, **d**eep **u**nderground **m**ountain **b**asing, for missile storage

CLODS, **C**omputerized **L**ogic-**O**riented **D**esign **S**ystem, Air Force

MISHAP, **Mis**siles **H**igh-Speed **A**ssembly **P**rogram

RETREAD, **Re**tiree **Tr**aining for **E**xtended **A**ctive **D**uty

***SATIRE**: **S**cientific **a**nd **T**echnical **I**nformation **Re**viewed and **E**xploited,* an Army publication

SPLASH, **s**hipboard **p**latforms for **l**anding **a**nd **s**ervicing **h**elicopters

IRATE, **i**nterim **r**emote **a**ir **t**erminal **e**quipment

JEST, **j**ungle **e**nvironmental **s**urvival **t**raining

CONGA, **c**ombat **o**perations, **n**aval **g**unfire **a**ctivity

BAMBI may seem inappropriate for a **ba**llistic **m**issile **b**ombardment **i**nterceptor. But some critics contend that such innocent-sounding names are chosen deliberately, to function as euphemisms.

Perhaps the most notorious military coinage was **WHAM**, for "**W**inning **H**earts **a**nd **M**inds," a Vietnam War propaganda pacification program whose acronym proved more accurate than the full name.

Even overseas, bureaucrats have their problems. In 1954, the **Bru**ssels **T**reaty **O**rganization just barely escaped the less-than-euphonious **BRUTO**. (In Italian, *brutto* means ugly.)

Certain technical acronyms raise the question: Is this what they really had in mind? Consider, for example:

SORDID, **S**ummary **o**f **R**eported **D**efects, **I**ncidents, and **D**elays

COMICS, **C**omputer-**O**riented **M**anaged **I**nventory **C**ontrol **S**ystem

SCAM, **S**ynchronous **C**ommunications **A**ccess **M**ethod

GEESE, **G**eneral **E**lectric **E**lectronic **S**ystem **E**valuator

SPOOF, **S**tructure and **P**arity **O**bserving **O**utput **F**unction

IDIOT, **I**ntrumentation **Di**gital **O**n-Line **T**ranscriber

OCCULT, **O**rdered **C**omputer **C**ollation of **U**nprepared **L**iterary **T**exts

BEAST, **B**rookings **E**conomic **a**nd **S**tatistical **T**ranslator

CADAVRS, **C**omputer-**A**ssisted **D**ial **A**ccess **V**ideo **R**etrieval **S**ystem

CANCER, **C**omputer **A**nalysis of **N**onlinear **C**ircuits **E**xcluding **R**adiation

NUTS, **N**ewcastle **U**niversity **T**eaching **S**ystem, England

ORDEAL, **O**ak **R**idge **D**ata **E**valuation and **A**nalysis **L**anguage

GOOF, **G**eneral **O**n-line **O**riented **F**unction

WAITS, **W**ide-**A**rea **I**nformation **T**ransfer **S**ystem

MESS, **M**echanical **E**lectronic **S**ubassembly **S**imulator

TRASH, **T**sunami **R**esearch **A**dvisory **S**ystem of **H**awaii

GAELIC, **G**rumman **A**erospace **E**ngineering **L**anguage for **I**nstructional **C**heckout

Companies sometimes assign internal working names to products, which are changed before marketing. A major software company temporarily called a product **G**eneral **L**anguage for **O**rdinary **P**eople, or **GLOP**.

More awkward coinages:

JEMIMA, **J**apan **E**lectric **M**easuring **I**nstruments **M**anufacturers **A**ssociation

HICCUP, **H**earing **I**mpaired **C**onsultants **C**reating **U**nique **P**artnerships

MIASMA, **M**ental **I**llness **A**ssociation, **S**ocial and **M**edical **A**spects

IDLE, **I**daho **D**epartment of **L**aw **E**nforcement

ADIOS, **A**utomatic **D**igital **I**nput-**O**utput **S**ystem

FATCAT, **F**ilm **a**nd **T**elevision **C**orrelation **A**ssessment **T**echnique

POSSUM, **P**olar **O**rbiting **S**atellite **S**ystem, **U**niversity of **M**ichigan

SANTA, **S**outh **A**frica **N**ational **T**uberculosis **A**ssociation

PANIC, **P**lanned **A**ttack on **N**ine **I**nner **C**ities, a program to build educational parks

HELL, **H**igher **E**ducation **L**earning **L**aboratory

MUD, a **m**unicipal **u**tility **d**istrict, supplying water to Austin, Tex., residents

MUDPIE, **M**useum and **U**niversity **D**ata **P**rocessing **I**nformation **E**xchange

CASH, **C**ommission for **A**dministrative **S**ervices in **H**ospitals

PITS, **P**acific **I**sland **T**raining **S**chool

GERBIL, the **G**reat **E**ducation **R**eform **Bil**l, legislation in the United Kingdom, 1988

SLOB, **S**ecured-**L**ease **O**bligation **B**onds, *and* **S**atellite **L**ow **O**rbit **B**ombardment

From an Environmental Protection Agency glossary: **SLAM** (**S**tate/**L**ocal **A**ir **M**onitoring Station) and **SNARL** (**s**uggested **n**o **a**dverse **r**esponse **l**evel), a measurement of the safety of drinking water.

A charitable employee program run by the Coors brewery in Colorado is called **V**olunteers **in** **C**ommunity Enrichment. Instead of ignoring or changing the somewhat inapropos name, the company exploits the double meaning by calling its program "the **VICE** Squad."

Some acronyms are not particularly negative but do seem to be peculiar choices. For instance, we wonder about . . .

GEISHA, **G**un **E**lectron-**I**nduced **S**emiconductor **H**ybrid **A**mplifier

DOMESTIC, **D**evelopment **o**f **M**inicomputers in an **E**nvironment of **S**cientific and **T**echnological **I**nformation **C**enters

PASSION, **P**rogram for **A**lgebraic **S**equences **S**pecifically of **I**nput-**O**utput **N**ature

HOT-DAM, **H**igher **O**rder **T**ree **D**ual **A**pproximation **M**ethod

BAMBAM, **B**ook **A**lert: **M**issing **B**ooks **a**nd **M**anuscripts, a computer network that recalls *The Flintstones*

SERAPHIM, **S**ystems **E**ngineering **R**especting **A**cquisition and **P**ropagation of **H**euristic **I**nstructional **M**aterials, a chemistry term

WAMPUM, **W**age **a**nd **M**anpower **P**rocess **U**tilizing **M**achines, at the Bureau of Indian Affairs payroll office in Albuquerque; WAMPUM is also **W**artime **A**vailability of **M**edical **P**ersonnel **U**pon **M**obilization.

Finally in our section on infelicitous acronymy, some especially impolite consequences. Consider, for example, NASA's reputed **S**aturn **l**aunch **u**mbilical **t**ower.

I.B.M.'s **F**orward **E**rror **C**ontrol **E**lectronics **S**ystem was hastily renamed **DACOR**, for **da**ta **cor**rection.

Although innocent in English, some acronyms can acquire negative meanings in other languages. Such as **FEA**, for **F**ederal **E**nergy **A**dministration. In Spanish, *fea* means ugly. Perhaps that's why, in 1977, the agency became the Department of Energy.

Some alleged blunders, however, are apocryphal and facetious. Don't bother trying to register for classes at the mythical **S**am **H**ouston **I**nstitute of **T**echnology. And the ever-popular but nonexistent **F**irst **U**nitarian **C**hurch, **K**ennebunkport, **ME** will never hold Sunday services. (Thank heavens!)

Proper Names

The use of initials is commonplace, from writers **G.B.S.** (**G**eorge **B**ernard **S**haw) and **F.P.A.** (**F**ranklin **P**ierce **A**dams) to recent presidents such as **F.D.R.**, **J.F.K.**, and **L.B.J.**

The letter pseudonyms of some literary folk are more famous than their real names.

Hilda **D**oolittle (1886–1961), an American poet, was universally known as **H.D.**, her pen name. George William Russell (1867–1935), Irish poet and essayist, used the letters **A.E.** (sometimes rendered with a ligature: Æ) as his signature. The initials are said to be a printer's error, a misreading of his intended pseudonym **Ae**on (an early spelling of eon, suggesting age or eternity). Writer and missionary Charlotte Maria Tucker (1821–93) chose the more acronymic **A.L.O.E.**, for **A** **L**ady **o**f **E**ngland.

During the Middle Ages, acronymic names were common among Jews, especially rabbis. Some familiar Jewish surnames originated as acronyms, such as **Brill**, which may be a condensation of **B**en (son of) **R**abbi **Y**ehuda **L**evi.

"Sometimes parents neglect to note that the initials of the name form a word," says onomastics expert Elsdon C. Smith in his *Treasury of Name Lore.*

It's hardly surprising that **A**rthur **S**eymour **S**ullivan (of Gilbert and Sullivan fame) disliked his initials, according to Hesketh Pearson, one of the team's many biographers. On the other hand, writes Smith, "in many parts of England and among [black American families] a name is considered to be lucky if its initials form a word." Some Cambodian kids have been named **Untac** by parents appreciative of the work of the **U**nited **N**ations **T**ransitional **A**uthority, **C**ambodia.

According to one story, a lawyer named **D**aniel **A**shton **M**artin hired a secretary named **I**rene **T**hompson, resulting in a distinctive subscript for the attorney's business correspondence.

The parents of a child born in England in 1876

chose to give him the creative name **L**yulph **Y**dwallo **O**din **N**estor **E**gbert **L**yonel **T**oedmag **H**ugh **E**rchenwyne **S**axon **E**sa **C**romwell **O**rma **N**evill **D**ysart. It all spells out **LYONEL THE SECOND**. Lyulph passed on in 1961, according to *Debrett's Illustrated Peerage,* which notes that he had a few other names, too.

In *Finnegans Wake,* wordplay enthusiast James Joyce presents a strangely similar but not identical string of names. We shall spare you the full list, but it forms the acronym **HERE COMES EVERYBODY**. The names had long puzzled readers of Joyce (not an unusual occurrence). Then, in a 1984 journal article, Bernard Benstock, a professor at the University of Tulsa, pointed out the Dysart coincidence and speculated that Joyce may have found inspiration for the mountainous monicker in *Debrett's* or a newspaper item about the volume.

The acronym further reduces to **H.C.E.**, the initials of **H**umphrey **C**himpden **E**arwicker, the "hero" of *Finnegans Wake.* These three initials appear in the novel literally thousands of times, and Joyce gives them a host of alternative expansions and meanings.

Viewers of *Dick Van Dyke Show* reruns will recall the episode in which his son Ritchie discovers to his horror that his middle name is **Rosebud**—an acronym for the names of seven relatives.

Some initials create "initialism words," a phenomenon discussed earlier. **K.C.** is **Casey**, for example. **Arjay** Miller, former president of the Ford

Motor Company, received his name from his father's initials. At the height of her fame, **B**rigitte **B**ardot was affectionately known to French-speaking audiences as **B.B.**, letters homophonous in French with ***bébé***. The artist **Erté** (1892–1990) devised his famous signature from the French pronunciation of the initials of his original name: **R**omain de **T**irtoff.

Until recently, boats, ships, and hurricanes were most often given female names. Distaff appellations are also popular for acronyms.

When Britain declared war on Germany in 1914, the **D**efence **o**f the **R**ealm **A**cts, or **DORA**, imposed numerous restrictions on the public. The inconveniences were resented, and "Dora" was pictured in cartoons as a grouchy, elderly woman.

CAROL (**C**omputer **A**ssisted **R**esearch **O**n-**L**ine), meet **DORIS** (**D**irect **O**rder **R**ecording and **I**nvoicing **S**ystem) and **MARGIE** (**M**emory **A**nalysis **R**esponse **G**eneration and **I**nterface in **E**nglish). **ALICE** (**A**pplicative **L**anguage **I**dealized **C**omputing **E**ngine), meet **AMANDA** (**A**utomatized **M**edical **An**amnesis **D**ialog **A**ssistant) and **CARLA** (**C**ode **A**ctuated **R**andom **L**oad **A**pparatus).

Have **CLARA** (**C**omputerized **L**oad **a**nd **R**esource **A**nalysis) and **DIANE** (**D**istance **I**ndicating **A**utomatic **N**avigating **E**quipment) been introduced? How about **ELLA** (**E**uropean **L**ong **L**ines **A**gency), **EMMA** (**E**ye **M**ovement **M**easuring **A**pparatus), **LOLITA** (**L**ibrary **O**n-**L**ine **I**nformation and **T**ext **A**ccess), **PATRICIA** (**P**ractical **A**lgorithm **t**o **R**eceive

Information **C**oded **in** **A**lphanumeric), and **ROSIE** (**R**ooters **O**rganized to **S**timulate **I**nterest and **E**nthusiasm)?

SARA (**S**ociety of **A**merican **R**egistered **A**rchitects) should know **RACHEL** (**R**andom **A**ccess **C**hemical **H**azards **E**lectronic **L**ibrary) and, visiting from Britain, **TESSA** (**T**ax-**E**xempt **S**pecial **S**avings **A**ccount).

What does it all mean? Perhaps it just proves that there is nothing like a **DAME** (**D**ata **A**cquisition and **M**onitoring **E**quipment)—or a **DAMSEL** (**D**irectory of **A**ustralian **M**anufactured **S**cientific **E**quipment and **L**aboratoryware).

Acronymic Epithets and Slurs, Real and Mythical

Derogatory and insulting names for various disliked groups, ethnic and otherwise, are sometimes acronymic.

A **SAM** is a **S**outhern **A**ppalachian **M**igrant. **TOM** is used by rural Canadians to deride city slickers in **T**oronto, **O**ttawa, and **M**ontreal. **JAP**, for **J**ewish **A**merican **P**rincess, is used jokingly, but is still offensive to many. In Chapter 4, we discussed **Wasp** and **yuppie**.

Also in that chapter, we examined words mistakenly alleged to be acronyms. Here are four more.

The epithet **wop** (1912 or earlier) is reputed to be from **w**ith**o**ut **p**assport or **w**ithout **o**fficial **p**apers, phrases supposedly stamped on immigrants' documents. In another version, the laborer **w**orks **o**n **p**avement. More probable is that wop is a clipping and Anglicization of *guappo,* Neapolitan dialect meaning a ruffian or tough guy. Some commentators suggested that President Johnson's much-touted "**W**ar **o**n **P**overty" was handicapped by its name from the outset. (In World War II British military slang, wop *was* an acronym—for **w**ireless **op**erator.)

Among the British, a foreigner, especially an Arab or Indian, was often called a **wog** (1929). Usually disparaging, it's often said to stand for "**w**ily [or **w**orthy or **w**onderful or **W**esternized] **O**riental **g**entleman." Yet another acronymic interpretation is that **WOGS** was an abbreviation used by British authorities for local employees: **w**orking **o**n **g**overnment **s**ervice. *The Oxford English Dictionary* glosses the word in these cautious terms: "Origin uncertain: often said to be an acronym, but none of the many suggested etymologies is satisfactorily supported by the evidence." Several lexicographers say it's a clipping of "golliwogg," the name of a grotesque black doll with frizzy hair that was popularized in a series of late-nineteenth-century children's stories.

A similarly xenophobic term, applied by Australians to English immigrants, was **pommy** or **pommie** or **pom** (late nineteenth century). This epithet is said to dervive from **POME**, **P**risoner **o**f **M**other **E**ngland, or **POHM**, **P**risoner **o**f **H**is **M**ajesty, both referring to the convicts exiled to Australia's penal colonies. Not likely, but an alternative origin has been proposed: Australian children, seeking a rhyme for immigrant, clipped *pomegranate*, a red fruit that reminded them of the easily sunburned English.

"**T**he **w**oman **i**s **r**equested to **p**ay," an announcement at school dances, supposedly gave birth to another derisive appellation: **twirp** (1925 or earlier), a male unable to afford a date. *The Oxford English Dictionary* says "of uncertain origin" but cites another possible alphabetical etymology: the name of **T. W. Earp**, a student at Exeter College, Oxford, who graduated in 1911. Mr. Earp's abilities and achievements were apparently so spectacular that they provoked envy among his classmates. Yet another etymology suggests that the word is a variant of *twit*. An alternative spelling for this nerd of yesteryear is *twerp*.

A slur can be turned on its ear via humorous redefinition. In the 1960s, when some angry young protesters shouted "**pig!**" at police officers (an epithet that goes back to the early nineteenth century), the cops struck back by displaying bumper stickers claiming the word stands for "**p**ride, **i**ntegrity, **g**uts."

Titles and Honors

We earlier noted that fraternal groups love impressive- and mystical-sounding titles with ancient roots, such as "**T**hrice **I**llustrious and **P**uissant **G**rand **M**aster," abbreviated as **T.I.P.G.M.** Science fiction and fantasy buffs have adopted this custom, no doubt with a smile—for example, a "**S**ecret **M**aster **o**f **G**aming" is a **SMOG**.

Years ago, it was more common for professionals to append to their names the initials of titles or memberships. But if you were a **M**ember of the **I**nstitute of **C**ivil **E**ngineers, you might be reluctant to sign yourself John Smith, **MICE**. A similar problem would confront a **M**ember of the **O**rganization and **M**ethods **S**ociety (United Kingdom), or a **B**achelor of **A**rts in **S**ocial **S**cience.

Across the Atlantic, wags have irreverently redefined the abbreviations of certain British titles, which also follow proper names. A **C**ommander of the Order of St. **M**ichael and St. **G**eorge is shortened to **C.M.G.**, which really means, we are told, "**C**all **M**e **G**od." A **K**night **C**ommander of St. **M**ichael and St. **G**eorge is **K.C.M.G.**, which announces "**K**indly **C**all **M**e **G**od." And a Knight of the **G**rand **C**ross of St. **M**ichael and St. **G**eorge, **G.C.M.G.**, signifies—what else?—"**G**od **C**alls **M**e **G**od."

Geographical Acronyms

A major nation is an acronym.

For centuries, Moslems in India had sought their own country. By combining words from Hindustani and Urdu, the name *Pakistan,* meaning "land of the pure" or "holy country," was suggested for such a new country.

Coincidentally enough, the names of some of the

northwestern Indian provinces that were most heavily Moslem—**P**unjab, the **A**fghan border states, **K**ashmir, **S**ind, and Baluchis**tan**—formed a quasi-acronym of **Pakistan**. A national homeland composed of these areas was formally proposed in 1930 by Muhammad Iqbāl, a philosopher and poet. In 1933, the coincidence was noted by Chaudrie Rahmat Ali. When Great Britain granted independence to India in 1947, the long-sought state was born. (As it turned out, Kashmir remained under the control of India.)

But Pakistan isn't alone. **Tanzania** was created from **Tan**ganyika and **Zan**zibar in 1964. A proposed union of the South Pacific countries **Ma**laysia, the **Phil**ippines, and **Indo**nesia would be called **Maphilindo**.

Still other geographical names, or *toponyms*, are syllabic acronyms or blends, including **BENELUX** (**Be**lgium, the **Ne**therlands, and **Lux**embourg), **DELMARVA** (**Del**aware, **Mar**yland, and **V**irgini**a**), and the trendy Manhattan neighborhoods **SoHo** (**So**uth of **Ho**uston Street) and **Tribeca** (**Tri**angle **be**low **Ca**nal Street).

Reston, Va., was named for founder **R**obert **E.** **S**imons, plus **ton**, a suffix for town. **Texarkana**, situated near the borders of **Tex**as, **Ark**ansas, and Louisi**ana**, was in the spotlight in 1992 as the home of independent presidential candidate H. Ross Perot. And **Calneva** Drive in West Los Angeles is a combination of **Cal**ifornia and **Neva**da.

Acronyms proposed for America's sprawling

"supercities" include **BOSNYWASH** and **BOSWASH** (**Bos**ton and **Wash**ington, with or without **N**ew **Y**ork), **CHIPITTS** (**Chi**cago and **Pitts**burgh), and **SANSAN** (**San** Francisco and **San** Diego).

Because the word *American* can apply to other citizens of the Western Hemisphere, an unambiguous replacement has been sought. One suggestion is **Usan** (pronounced "YOO-san"), which turns the initials **U.S.A.** into an acronym.

Time for a Change

Suppose officials of a corporation or organization decide to change its name. But they wish to preserve the familiarity and "equity" that the abbreviation of the existing name has acquired. So management chooses a *new* name that consists of the *same* series of letters as the older one. If the company has invested heavily in monogrammed golf shirts, this strategy can save big bucks.

Let's look at a few examples of this process.

Originally, Jesse Jackson's **PUSH** organization meant **P**eople **U**nited to **S**ave **H**umanity. The **S** was subsequently redefined as **S**erve. Based in Elmhurst, Ill., **FEMALE** originally meant **F**ormerly **E**mployed **M**others **a**t **L**oose **E**nds. Now, more positively, it is **F**ormerly **E**mployed **M**others **at** the **L**eading **E**dge.

TCBY, the initialism of the franchised snack shop chain, originally stood for "**T**his **C**an't **B**e **Y**ogurt!" It was subsequently redefined as "**T**he **C**ountry's **B**est

Yogurt." One of the reasons may have been to avoid confusion with the competitive chain that exclaims "I Can't Believe It's Yogurt!"

A name change may create peculiar consequences for the resulting acronym. **UNICEF** originally meant **U**nited **N**ations **I**nternational **C**hildren's **E**mergency **F**und. Shedding two components, it became United Nations Children's Fund. But the organization continues to use the old acronym.

Some companies solve the problem of an obsolete name by going a step farther: They retain the letters but *abandon the expansion entirely*—or so they say.

CARE, originally **C**ooperative for **A**merican **R**emittances to **E**urope, went through several transformations. Europe became **E**verywhere, Remittances became **R**elief. Today, officials say they just CARE.

CBS, it seems, is just that, and no longer the **C**olumbia **B**roadcasting **S**ystem. **R**obotic **V**ision **S**ystems, **I**nc., when it abandoned robot manufacturing, changed its name to **RVSI**. In the wake of cholesterol concern and fat fright, **K**entucky **F**ried **C**hicken is now (the company insists) plain old **KFC**.

Also on the list of companies that have adopted an "initials only" policy are **NCR** (formerly **N**ational **C**ash **R**egister), **TRW** (formerly **T**hompson-**R**amo-**W**ooldridge), and **GAF** (once **G**eneral **A**niline and **F**ilm). Across the Atlantic, what used to be **B**ritish **H**ome **S**tores is now just **BHS**.

After this sort of transformation, periods, if they existed previously, are usually dropped, presumably because they would only draw even more attention to the question of what the letters represent.

The position of these institutions, in effect, is that *no* expansions exist for their names. That claim may be plausible when (as in the case of CARE) the name is an acronym synonymous with a preexisting word. Then the name remains meaningful even after the change. But with a plain old *initialism,* it seems odd to declare that, for example, **TRW** stands for nothing at all.

Perhaps the ultimate statement on this trend is the Boulder, Colo., computer firm that, on its founding in 1973, called itself **NBI**. According to a spokesperson, company lore is that the name stands for **n**othing **b**ut **i**nitials. (I attempted unsuccessfully to track down a firm allegedly named **SOLFAM**, for "**s**ick **o**f **l**ooking **f**or **a** **n**ame.")

Sometimes a change solves one problem but inadvertently creates another. In 1991, the **A**ssociation for **R**etarded **C**itizens, citing the stigma of the word "retarded," elected to change its name to "The **Arc**," from the acronym created by its name. But the organization's officials apparently failed to realize that **ARC** carries its own pejorative connotations, as an acronym for "**A**IDS-**R**elated **C**omplex."

A Revolutionary Renaming

Sometimes the consequences of this process can be historic.

The initialism **U.S.S.R.** stands for **U**nion of **S**oviet

Socialist **R**epublics. In Cyrillic, the letters of the Russian words *Soyuz Sovetskikh Sotsialisticheskikh Respublik* are rendered as C.C.C.P. In May 1991, following the crumbling of Socialist-Communist systems around the globe and separatist rumblings in the Baltic nations, then-President Gorbachev and leaders of the republics tentatively agreed to change the name of the federation.

"Socialist" was to become "Sovereign," thus retaining the familiar initials in both Cyrillic and English. At the time, *The New York Times* called the abandonment of the word socialist "a remarkable step in the collapse of Communism."

But even more remarkable events were to follow. Later that year, the Union collapsed completely and some of the newly free nations joined in the informal **C**ommonwealth of **I**ndependent **S**tates. The awkward initialism is **C.I.S.** in English; in Russian the name is ***S**odruzhestvo **N**ezavisimykh **G**osudarstv,* or **S.N.G.**

The Russian word *sneg* means snow. In December 1991, this seemed apropos, and inspired some Russians to comment with bitter irony that the new government might melt by spring.

Here in the U.S.A., the problem of what to call the confederation seemed insoluble. Some American scientists began referring to the **F**ormer **S**oviet **U**nion, or **F.S.U.** What was the reaction at **F**lorida **S**tate **U**niversity in Tallahassee? "We love it!" exclaimed an official.

As 1991 drew to a close, a tongue-in-cheek list of

suggestions appeared in *The Foreign Observer,* a magazine published at Johns Hopkins University. It evidently struck a chord, and was quoted and reprinted in other publications. Among the more ingenious candidates: **B**olshevik-**O**rganized **R**epublic of **I**ndependent **S**tates (**BORIS**), **C**onfederation **o**f **M**oslem **M**onarchies and **I**ndependent **E**uropean **S**tates (**COMMIES**), and **R**ussian **U**nion of **B**olshevik-**L**ed **E**uropean **S**tates (**RUBLES**).

CHAPTER 7

❖

Foreign-Language Abbreviations Generate Pursuit Of Linguistic Eclecticism (FLAGPOLE)

So far, our explorations have focused almost exclusively on English. How prevalent are acronyms in other languages?

Every language with an alphabet employs abbreviations. And as we have seen, some abbreviations English speakers use are borrowings from other tongues.

Foreign-language abbreviations are often in the news—sometimes without expansion or explanation. For example:

F.A.L.N. is ***F****uerzas* ***A****rmadas de* ***L****iberación* ***N****acional,* or Armed Forces of National Liberation. It's the name of revolutionary groups in both Venezuela and Puerto Rico.

POLISARIO stands for *(Frente)* ***Po****pular para la* ***Li****beración de* ***Sa****guia el Hamra y* ***Rio*** *de Oro,* a guerrilla group fighting for the independence of the two indicated zones of the Western Sahara.

FRELIMO, ***Fre**nte de **Li**bertaçao de **Mo**çambique,* is the Portuguese name for Mozambique's Marxist ruling party.

Unita is also Portuguese, for ***U**nião **N**acional para a **I**ndependencia **T**otal de **A**ngola.*

Cross-culturally, acronyms can be tricky. The **C**anadian **E**xecutive **S**ervice **O**rganization, or **CESO**, a volunteer agency, pronounces it "KAY-so." But not in Latin America, where the name becomes a homophone for *queso,* cheese in Spanish. To avoid the bilingual pun, a soft C is substituted.

Here is an acronymic world tour.

Russian

Some Russian acronyms are familiar to us, and a few have become part of our own vocabulary.

The word ***agitprop*** is a syllabic acronym derived from the Russian words ***agit**atsiya **prop**aganda,* which are similar to their English counterparts.

Other acronym-derived Russian words that many Americans know:

The Moscow department store ***GUM*** (***G**osudarstvenni **U**niversalni **M**agazin*), Universal State Store; ***AMTORG*** (***Am**erikanskaya **torg**ovlya*), the American Trading Organization, which for many years provided cover for espionage activity;

and the luxury car ***Zil*** (***Z****avod* ***I****meni* ***L****ikhacheva*), "factory named for Likhachev."

TASS (***T****elegraphnoye* ***A****gentsvo* ***S****ovyetskovo* ***S****oyuza*), Telegraph Agency of the Soviet Union, is now the friendlier **RITA** (***R****ossiyskoye* ***I****nformatsionno-****T****elegraphnoye* ***A****gentsvo*), the Russian Information Telegraph Agency.

Speaking of TASS, one of their dispatches in 1984 noted that Russians have "a passion for every kind of abbreviation and short designation." One reason is that many institutional names are long.

Consider the ***S****ibirskii* ***N****auchno-****I****ssledovatel'skii* ***I****nstitut* ***G****eologii* ***G****eofiziki* ***i*** ***M****ineral'nogo* ***S****yr'ya* (whew!), which means "Siberian Scientific Research Institute of Geology, Geophysics, and Mineral Raw Materials." No wonder Russian-speakers prefer to call it "**SNIIGGIMS**" (pronounced "sneeee GEEMS," with a hard G). For an even *more* verbose Russian example, see page 253, where we consider the world record for length.

In the 1920s and 1930s, the vast and onerous Communist bureaucracy generated a plethora of acronyms, some of which are still familiar.

The original Soviet secret police, created by Lenin in 1917, was the ***Cheka***, from ***Ch****rezvychainaya* ***K****ommissiya po Borbe s Kontrrevolutsiei i Sabotazhem,* meaning Extraordinary Committee for Combating Counterrevolution and Sabotage. In 1923, it was succeeded by **OGPU** (sometimes just **G.P.U.**), from ***O****b'edinënnoe* ***G****osudárstvennoe* ***P****olitícheskoe* ***U****pravlénie,* or United State Political

Directorate. Less acronymic but no less fearsome, it became the **N.K.V.D.** in 1934, the **M.V.D.** in 1944, and the **K.G.B.** in 1954.

Although it may sound like something from spy fiction, ***SMERSH*** (noted briefly in Chapter 6) was real: a group of World War II Red Army secret police units assigned to monitor dissent. The name is generally interpreted as an acronym for ***Smert'*** ***Sh**pionam,* or "Death to spies!" But according to émigré journalist Kirill Khenkin, it was really based on the more unwieldy ***S**petsial'nie* ***Me**todi* ***R**azoblachenia* ***Sh**pionov,* meaning "special methods for exposing spies."

Alexander Solzhenitsyn's *The* ***Gulag*** *Archipelago* (1973) gave wide notoriety to the acronym for a network of forced-labor camps: ***G**lavnoye* ***u**pravleniye* *ispravitel'no-trudovykh* ***lag**erei,* or "main administration of corrective labor camps." (Solzhenitsyn's use of the word archipelago is metaphorical.)

SAMBO is not just a character in a now politically incorrect American children's story, but an acronym for ***Sam**ozashchita* ***be**z* ***o**ruzhiya,* or hand-to-hand combat. Literally, "self-defense without weapons."

The Soviet fighter plane known as a ***MiG*** was named for its designers: Artem **Mi**koyan, an Air Force officer, and Mikhail **G**urevich, a mathematician.

A trend among Russian parents in the former U.S.S.R. was to give their offspring patriotic names, often in creative acronymic form. One was **Vilior**, which stood for "**V**ladimir **Il**yich **Len**in, **I**nitiator of the **O**ctober **R**evolution." Syllabic variations on the theme included **Vladlen** and the more euphonious **Marlena**—not for Dietrich but for **Mar**x and **Len**in.

Melor Sturua, a prominent Moscow journalist, was originally named **Melsor,** for "**M**arx, **E**ngels, **L**enin, **S**talin, **O**ctober **R**evolution." When Stalin was officially declared a bad guy, Mr. Sturua dropped the "s." In 1989, friends joked that the way things were going in the U.S.S.R., he might gradually lose *all* the letters of his name.

German

German is an agglutinative language, receptive to compounding. The word for the study of economics, for example, is *Wirtschaftswissenschaft,* combining the words for economy and science. Syllabic acronyms thus come naturally. (Note that German nouns, acronymic or otherwise, are initial-capped.)

Some samples from World War II:

Nazi is from ***Na****tionalso****zi****alistische,* the name of the party.

Gestapo is from ***Ge****heime* ***Sta****ats****po****lizei,* the Secret State Police.

A prisoner-of-war camp for captured enemy officers was an ***Oflag,*** from ***Of****fizier* and ***Lag****er* (camp).

The plane called a ***Stuka*** was short for ***Stu***_rz_***ka***_mpfflugzeug,_ literally dive fighter, or what the Allies called a dive bomber.

The word ***flak*** originated in 1938 from ***Fl***_ieger-_***a***_bwehr_***k***_anone,_ literally "aircraft (or aviator) defense cannon," an antiaircraft gun. The original meaning was the weapon, then the shells ejected from the gun. In English, its metaphoric use for criticism ("taking a lot of flak") dates from the 1960s. (Don't confuse *flak* with *flack,* an insulting name for a publicist.)

As Germany began to lose the war, notes Cornelius Ryan in *The Last Battle,* Berliners sarcastically referred to Hitler as ***Gröfaz***, an abbreviation of ***Grö***_sseste_ ***F***_eldherr_ ***A***_lle_ ***Z***_eit_ ("Greatest General of All Time").

After the war, a secret plan to spirit Nazi war criminals out of the country and give them new identities was dubbed **ODESSA**, for ***O***_rganisation_ ***d***_er_ ***E***_hemaligen_ **S.S.** ***A***_ngehörigen,_ or Organization of Former Members of the S.S. (The **S.S.** was the elite ***S***_chutz_***s***_taffel,_ literally "protection squadron," whose members were the dreaded blackshirts.) The acronym is also a pun on Odessa, a Russian seaport. The name gained renewed attention in Frederick Forsyth's 1972 novel *The Odessa File,* and the 1974 film.

A Siemens computer software program is called ***g***_rosspeicher_***o***_rientierte_ ***l***_istenorganisierte_ ***E***_rmittlungs_***m***_ethode,_ or **GOLEM** for short. It translates as

"RAM (random access memory)-oriented list-based method." The name is an odd choice. In Jewish folklore, a *golem* is a kind of robot, a man-made servant who is supposed to be helpful but who causes trouble because it follows instructions too literally. That could apply to a lot of software!

French

You probably won't require translations for these.

An E.E.C. program that provides financial support to encourage collaboration among researchers in various countries in Europe is called ***S**timulation des **C**oopérations **I**nternationales et des **É**changes **N**écessaires aux **C**hercheurs **E**uropéennes,* or **SCIENCE.**

Among other French acronyms:

SESAME, ***S**tation d'**É**coute de **Sa**tellites de **Mé**térologiques*

PASCAL, ***P**rogramme **A**ppliqué à la **S**élection et à la **C**ompilation **A**utomatique de la **L**ittérature,* a national scientific bibliographic database

ANTIOPE, ***A**cquisition **N**umérique de **T**élévisualisation d'**I**mages **O**rganisées en **P**ages d'**É**criture,* a videotext service; Antiope was a personage in Greek mythology

AIDE, ***A**ction **I**nternationale pour les **D**roits de l'**E**nfant*

PARIS, ***P****our l'****A****ménagement et le* ***R****enouveau* ***In****stitutionnel et* ***S****ocial,* a political party

Other Languages

In Chapter 3, we noted that acronyms have a long history, with perhaps the earliest pure examples in Hebrew. The tradition continues. An Israeli movement opposing the country's financial dependence on the United States is called ***Ma****spik* ***'****im* ***S****hnor* ("Enough With Handouts"), or **MAAS**. The Hebrew letter *ayin* in the preposition *'im* creates the second vowel in the acronym. The coinage is appropriate, because *maas* is a Hebrew word that means activity or doing.

In 1842, during the *Risorgimento* (the word means revival or resurrection), the movement for Italian liberation and unification, a patriotic chorus in Giuseppe Verdi's opera *Nabucco* galvanized audiences. Nationalists then redefined the composer's surname as a codeword for ***V****ittorio* ***E****manuele,* ***Re*** ***d'I****talia,* and shouts of "*Viva* ***VERDI****!*" had a dual meaning. In 1861, Victor Emmanuel II did indeed become the first king of Italy.

E*thnikos* (or ***E****llinikos*) ***L****aikos* ***A****peleutherotikos* ***S****tratos,* the National (or Greek) Popular Liberation Army, forms the acronym **ELAS**. The Greek word for Greece is *Ellas*.

For samples of how speakers of other languages humorously rewrite abbreviations, see the next chapter.

CHAPTER 8

❖

Some Acronyms That Inevitably Require Existence (SATIRE)

The previous chapters have only occasionally revealed the amusement potential of the form. Now we turn seriously to the humorous side of the phenomenon.

Facetious Redefinitions

As has been noted, an acronym or initialism can have *more than one* expansion. And many do. With only twenty-six letters to work with, duplication and ambiguity are inevitable. From this fact, many of the funny possibilities of acronyms emerge.

Existing acronyms and initialisms can be redefined for serious reasons, as we saw at the conclusion of Chapter 6. But such redefinitions can serve another purpose: to make a witty, pointed, or cynical observation.

The supersecret **N**ational **S**ecurity **A**gency, or

N.S.A., really means, some veterans assure us, "**n**ever **s**ay **a**nything" or "**n**o **s**uch **a**gency." Some of the **C.I.A.**'s operations might suggest that the agency's name means "**c**aught **i**n the **a**ct." The **O.S.S.**, or **O**ffice of **S**trategic **S**ervices, America's spy department in World War II, was redefined as "**o**h, **s**o **s**ocial" because many of its officials had been recruited from prestigious corporations and Ivy League colleges.

In the summer of 1991, following the **B.C.C.I.** scandal, *The New York Times* reported: "Police and intelligence experts nicknamed B.C.C.I. the '**b**ank of **c**rooks and **c**riminals.'" Jay Leno warned: "**B**e **c**areful: **c**rooks **i**nside."

In 1992, John Michael McNamara, a suburban New York auto dealer, pleaded guilty to bilking **G**eneral **M**otors **A**cceptance **C**orporation of huge sums of money in a fraudulent loan scheme to finance vehicle purchases. Wags joked that **G.M.A.C.** stood for "**G**ive **M**cNamara **a**nother **c**ar."

Some broadcasting industry people insist that **N.T.S.C.**, a video initialism for **N**ational **T**elevision **S**tandards **C**ommittee, really means "**N**ever **t**he **s**ame **c**olor."

Is **NATO** "**n**o **a**ction; **t**alk **o**nly"? Does **laser** stand for "**l**ucrative **a**pproach to **s**upport **e**xpensive **r**esearch"? During the 1977 "energy crisis," *Boston Globe* columnist Susan Trausch suggested that **OPEC** might mean "**o**il **p**eople **e**njoying **C**adillacs."

The now-notorious **P.T.L.** Club variously claimed that the letters stood for "**P**raise **t**he **L**ord" and (less grammatically) "**P**eople **t**hat **l**ove." After the sex-and-money scandal toppled televangelists Jim and Tammy Bakker, irreverent wits suggested that the initialism meant "**P**reachers **t**hat **l**ust," "**P**ass **t**he **l**oot," or "**P**ay **t**he **l**ady."

Founded in 1670, **H**udson's **B**ay **C**ompany is the world's oldest corporation. In *Merchant Princes,* an authoritative history of the huge firm, Peter C. Newman notes that the initials **H.B.C.** were variously redefined as "**H**ungry **B**elly **C**ompany," "**H**orny **B**oys' **C**lub," and "**H**ere **B**efore **C**anada."

Word Ways, The Journal of Recreational Linguistics, reported that to residents of the Sunshine State, **CALIF** means "**C**ome **a**nd **l**ive **i**n **F**lorida." Bristling Floridians riposte that **FLA** stands for "**F**lee **L**os **A**ngeles."

"Certain abbreviations and acronyms add humor to the atmosphere of busy and stressful day-to-day medical practice," observes Dal Yoo, a Washington, D.C., physician. In an article in *Verbatim, The Language Quarterly,* he cites cynical redefinitions by staffers and medical students.

The familiar initialism **T.L.C.**, for **t**ender **l**oving **c**are, is sometimes "**t**otal **l**ack of **c**oncern." **D.R.G.**, or **d**iagnostic **r**elated **g**roup (used to determine federal payments for medical services), becomes "**d**amned **r**egulatory **g**overnment." A promising cancer treatment called **LEEP**, for **l**oop **e**lectrosurgical **e**xcision **p**rocedure, drew a caveat from one physician, who warned that it should *not* be interpreted to mean "**L**et's **e**xcise **e**very **p**atient!"

In the tumultuous 1960s, student protesters at the University of California at Berkeley slyly claimed that the irreverent message on their signs really meant "**F**reedom **U**nder **C**lark **K**err" (the university's chancellor).

U.S. Army becomes "**U**ncle **S**am **a**in't **r**eleased **m**e **y**et." **Navy** means "**N**ever **a**gain **v**olunteer **y**ourself." Service people have also fancifully redefined **AWOL** as "**A**fter **wo**men and **l**iquor" and "**A** **w**olf **o**n the **l**oose." (For customers of a Washington, D.C., retailer, it meant "**A**lmost **W**holesale **o**r **L**ess.")

Kids say **Adidas** means "**A**ll **d**ay **I** **d**ream **a**bout **s**ex." In fact, the company name *is* an acronym, albeit syllabic. It was coined in Germany in the 1920s from the name of the founder, Adolf ("**Adi**") **Das**sler.

To reckless drivers, a **stop** sign may mean "**S**tart **t**romping **o**n **p**edal" (among several other suggested expansions).

An old joke in this vein involves a farmer whose son is away at college. He explains higher education to his friend Sam. "The first degree you receive is a **B.S.** You know what that means." Sam nods. Next is the **M.S.** "**M**ore of the **s**ame." Finally, after years of study, the **Ph.D.** "What's that one?" asks Sam. "**P**iled **h**igher and **d**eeper."

Revenge of the Consumers

The process of acronymic redefinition offers a form of humorous revenge to citizens oppressed and exploited by faceless government agencies or corporations. Powerless to fight the system, they strike back with mockery and satire, in comments that show what they *really* think.

These disgruntled consumers spontaneously redefine corporate, organizational, and institutional names in fanciful ways, often with devastating impact. The target may be an acronym, an initialism, or a conventional institutional name. In each case, the component letters are redefined to create a new and barbed meaning.

For example:

Unhappy airline passengers suspect that **Delta** means "**D**oesn't **e**ven **l**eave **t**he **a**irport" or "**D**o **ev**erything **l**onger **t**hrough **A**tlanta" (the airline's hub). **TWA** has spawned a plethora of pejorative redefinitions, including "**T**ry **w**alking **a**cross," "**T**housands **w**andering **a**imlessly," "**T**o **w**ait **a**lways," and "**T**he **w**orst **a**irline." **USAir** is "**U**nfortunately, **s**till **A**llegheny [the airline's previous name] **i**n **r**eality."

Foreign carriers fare no better. **Alitalia**, we are told, is "**A**lways **l**ate **i**n **t**akeoff, **a**lways **l**ate **i**n **a**rriving." Similarly, **El Al** flights "**E**mbark **l**ate, **a**rrive **l**ate." **BOAC** (**B**ritish **O**verseas **A**irways **C**orporation, now British Airways) is "**B**ring **o**ver **A**merican **c**ash" and "**B**etter **o**n **a** **c**amel." **SABENA** is "**S**uch **a** **b**ad **e**xperience—**n**ever **a**gain!" **BWIA** (**B**ritish **W**est **I**ndian **A**irways) prompts some travelers to inquire "**B**ut **w**ill **i**t **a**rrive?" **Lufthansa** gets off easy by comparison, inspiring the suggestion "**L**et **u**s **f**ondle **t**he **h**ostess **a**nd **n**ot **s**ay **a**nything."

Some dissatisfied automobile owners claim that **Ford** means "**F**ix **o**r **r**eplace **d**aily" or "**F**ound **o**n **r**oad **d**ead," and that **Pinto** stands for "**P**ut **i**n **n**ew **t**ransmission **o**ften." **AUDI** is "**A**nother **u**seless **d**amn **i**mport," and **BMW** announces "**B**reak **m**y **w**indow." **FIAT** supposedly means "**F**ix **i**t **a**gain, **T**ony." (As we noted on page 160, FIAT really *is* an acronym.)

The conversation of frustrated Americans inventively and sardonically acronymizes the names of sports teams such as the Indianapolis **Colts** ("**C**ount **o**n a **l**oss **t**his **S**unday"). **YMCA** means "**Y**our **m**oney **c**heerfully **a**ccepted." Consumer products can't escape—for example, **Tab** ("**T**otally **a**rtificial **b**everage").

The most battered victim of acronymic assault? Without a doubt, **I.B.M.**

The earliest example may be "**I**'ve **b**een **m**oved!," the chronic complaint of frequently transferred executives. When microcomputers began proliferating, the game took off uncontrollably. The most repeated examples: "**I**ncredibly **b**oring **m**achine" and "**I** **b**ought **M**acintosh." Other nominees include: "**I**nferior **b**ut **m**arketable," "**I**nspiring **b**itter **m**emories," "**I**ndustry's **b**iggest **m**istake," "**I**mbeciles **b**ecome **m**anagers," and "**I**t's **b**etter **m**anually." This is a small sampling from literally hundreds, some even more vicious.

Why Do We Do It?

Félix Rodríguez González, whom we have quoted before, calls the process under examination "the re-interpretation of initials and their playful function in the service of irony and jest."

Alleen Nilsen and Don L. F. Nilsen, humor scholars at Arizona State University, call the phenomenon "tendentious humor." Such jokes "are tendentious both in the Freudian sense of expressing hostility and in the dictionary sense of 'advancing a definite point of view.' "

In an excellent article in *The Journal of American Folklore* titled "Rewriting Initialisms: Folk Derivations and Linguistic Riddles," Nicholas Howe, a professor of English at Ohio State University, cites and analyzes scores of these jokes, giving us some insight into their purposes.

"That there are official and folk derivations for the same initialism [or acronym or word] demonstrates the existence of two varieties of language: one that is neither understood nor trusted, and one that is believed and enjoyed." The alternative expansion or hidden meaning, says Professor Howe, "conflicts with the accepted or official interpretation and thus subverts cultural norms." The facetious redefinition thus "expresses a proud and satiric refusal to accept the official."

Professor Howe classifies this kind of satiric wordplay as a type of *riddle,* a form of humor with a long history and deep significance for students of psychology and the social sciences. Because an abbreviation possesses two or more possible expansions (the official and the facetious), this riddling question is inevitably posed: "What words do these initial letters *really* stand for?" In practice, of course, the joke isn't always presented in the form of a question or a riddle. But Professor Howe's analysis is nevertheless provocative.

Facetious Redefinition in Other Tongues

The phenomenon of coining mocking reinterpretations of acronyms and initialisms is universal.

For generations of beleaguered Russians, derisive acronyms have been a subtle tool of scorn. Mandatory civil defense training, for example, was called ***grob***, a truncation of ***gr****azhdanskaya* ***ob****orona,* civil defense. *Grob* is the Russian word for coffin. Similarly, the military title ***Zam****estitel'* ***Kom****issara* ***po*** ***Mor****skim* ***De****lam,* or Deputy Secretary of Naval Affairs, was facetiously truncated to the syllabic acronym ***zamkom po morde***, which implies "I hit you in the face with a padlock."

The fabled eroticism of Gallic humor extends to alphabetic punnery. A button on an eighteenth-century man's coat was inscribed with the letters **L A C D**. In French, the pronunciation of the individual letters is homophonous with the phrase ***Elle a cédé***, "She has given in."

An Italian school is called ***I****stituto* ***T****ecnico* ***I****ndus-*

*triale **S**uperiore,* or **ITIS**. The acronym itself is meaningless in Italian. But at rival schools, students whimsically expand it to mean "***I**nutile **T**entare **I**struirli—**S**cemi!,*" or "It's futile to try to teach them; they're dumb!"

Wolfgang Schmidt, an athlete who fled East Germany before the fall of the Berlin Wall, relates in his 1991 book *Thrown Free* how those hoping to emigrate would bitterly recast the initials of ***D**eutsche **D**emokratische **R**epublik* as ***D**er **D**umme **R**est,* or "the stupid ones who are left behind."

In Poland's parliament, a rightist representative, addressing his formerly Communist colleagues, referred to the **P.Z.P.R.**, the initials of the defunct Polish United Workers Party (***P**olska **Z**jednoczona **P**artia **R**obotnicza*), as "***p**łatni **z**drajcy, **p**achołki **R**osji,*" or "paid traitors, Russia's flunkeys."

The Israeli Defense Force, ***Z**va **H**agana **L**'Israel,* is known by the initialism **Z.H.L.** and the acronym ***Zahal***. But some say it really stands for ***Z**rikhot **H**ayinu **L**'hitkhaten,* or "We should have gotten married." A woman who weds can be released from military service.

A Long Tradition

Humorous acronymic coinages and redefinitions may be as old as the phenomenon of abbreviation itself.

S.P.Q.R., the Roman initialism discussed on page 82, has also been "**S**mall **p**rofits, **q**uick **r**eturns" since at least the early 1900s. In 1831, New York cynics reinterpreted academic degrees, so **LL.D.** became "**L**icense to **L**ie **D**amnably." As far back as 1513, according to one account, facetious sentences were crafted from the characters for Roman numerals.

This kind of activity can, however, be carried to tasteless and offensive extremes.

When the *Challenger* space shuttle exploded in 1986, devotees of sick humor redefined **NASA** to mean "**N**eed **a**nother **s**even **a**stronauts" and "**N**eed **a**nother **s**huttle **a**lso." My research turned up other equally cruel examples, some racist, as well as homophobic redefinitions of AIDS. Because they are more vicious than amusing, we shall go no further.

More Humorous Acronymic Coinages

Have you heard about the **A.A./A.A.A.**? It's a new group for drunk drivers.

Another technique is the creation of *new* humorous acronyms. The object is often the same: to poke fun or score a point. The difference is that ordinary words are reworked into acronymic form. The process above is reversed: Instead of redefining the names of *existing* institutions, or whatever, the humorist creates *fictitious* ones.

Philadelphia writer Linda Morrison, in a 1987 newspaper article lambasting proposals to build expensive convention centers, suggested that the few who stand to profit from such boondoggles must belong to an elite club called "**L**eaders **o**f **O**ur **T**own"—more appropriately, **LOOT**.

In a letter to *The New York Times,* William Banks of Manhattan describes his anguished experience being subjected to the cacophony of early-morning trash collectors. They may, he wryly suggested, be representatives of the "**D**epartment for **E**xpanding and **A**mplifying **F**earsome **E**veryday **N**oises," or **DEAFEN**.

In another letter, James Frawley of Boonton Township, N.J., objects to the airlines' method of routing passengers through inconvenient connecting cities, which he describes as the "**H**ub **a**nd **S**poke **S**ystem of **L**evitating **E**verything," or **HASSLE**.

Columnist Russell Baker, decrying the excesses of political advertising, carps: "This is the commercial that won the prestigious **FAT PATT,** or **F**ooling **A**ll **T**he **P**eople **A**ll **T**he **T**ime award."

Writing in the regrettably defunct English humor magazine *Punch,* Alistair Beaton characterized a certain kind of tabloid headline as a **ZINGER**, which he explained means "**Z**eitgeist **i**ndicator **n**astily **g**enerating **e**xtreme **r**eactions." Beaton observes that "a zinger has to be pithy and provocative. . . . It has to catch the spirit of the times."

Fictitious organizations of recent years include **L**et **O**ral **R**oberts **D**ie (**LORD**), and **M**others **A**gainst **D**yslexia (**DAM**). Britons nicknamed Margaret

Thatcher **Tina** because of her repeated pronouncement: "There **i**s **n**o **a**lternative."

In response to Gerald Ford's 1976 **WIN** (**W**hip **I**nflation **N**ow) campaign, the National Taxpayers Union sent its members a button reading "**L**et's **o**ppose **s**tupid **e**xpenditures."

Gary Alexander, a Reston, Va., writer and editor, has formulated a set of acronymic maxims in the style of "Murphy's Law." My favorite is "The quieter you speak, the more importance will be ascribed to your opinions." He calls this rule the "**I**nverse **D**ecibel **I**ndex **o**f **T**ruth," or **IDIOT.**

To the familiar office initialism **T.G.I.F.**, or "**T**hank **G**od **I**t's **F**riday," one wag responded, "**P**hooey **o**n **e**verything, **t**omorrow's **S**aturday," or **POETS**. For those so eager for the weekend to arrive that they get their dates confused: "**S**o **h**appens [or **S**orry, **h**oney] **it**'s **T**hursday." These people may be fed up with **WOMBAT** (**w**aste **o**f **m**oney, **b**rains, **a**nd **t**ime) assignments. Or they might work for a boss with the irreverent job title: "**A**ssistant **S**taff **S**upervisor and **H**ead of **O**ther **L**ame **E**mployees."

At one time or another, this sort of game has probably been played in every workplace. Several anthologies reproducing such office humor and "urban folklore" have been published.

Similar silliness goes on in academia. In the late 1960s, a group of West Virginia teachers decided to poke fun at bureaucratic language by devising the "**R**edirected **U**nilateral and **M**ultifaceted **P**lans to **E**levate **L**ower **S**trata and **T**imid **I**ndividuals and to

Liven and **T**rain **S**cared **K**ids **in** **N**eed" . . . or **RUMPELSTILTSKIN**. And Henry H. Adams invented "**P**rofessors **L**eading the **U**ndergraduate-**G**raduate **U**nion of **G**reat **L**iberal **Y**earnings," or **PLUG-UGLY.**

Such coinages can boast distinguished practitioners. In 1838, Edgar Allan Poe (who also penned a few poems in acrostic form) satirized pseudo-intellectual societies by creating the "**P**hiladelphia, **R**egular, **E**xchange, **T**ea, **T**otal, **Y**oung, **B**elles, **L**ettres, **U**niversal, **E**xperimental, **B**ibliographical, **A**ssociation, **T**o, **C**ivilize, **H**umanity," or **P.R.E.T.T.Y.B.L.U.E.B.A.T.C.H.** "We all sign the initials of the society after our names," notes Psyche Zenobia, the group's fictitious corresponding secretary. (Punctuation per Poe's preference.)

In 1958, *Mad Magazine* published a panoramic cartoon panel in which dozens of people on a small-town main street are conversing entirely in acronyms. A cruising playboy-type says with a leer, "I belong to **WOLF**: **W**orshipers **o**f **L**onely **F**emales." His target is a member of **CUTE**: **C**oeds **U**nder **T**wenty-**e**ight. Suddenly a prudish matron intervenes: "On your way, young man! I belong to **STOP**, the **S**ociety **to** **O**utlaw **P**ickups."

When I began research for this book, I vividly recalled this article from my childhood—a tribute to *Mad*'s powerful influence on writers who grew up in its heyday.

In 1984, *Mad* returned to the genre in a feature

titled "Acronyms You Never Knew Existed." A few samples:

A new television **SEASON** features "**S**uperficial **e**ntertainment **a**nnually **s**een **o**n **n**etworks."

In a garage, a **TUNE-UP** becomes "**T**earing **u**p **n**ew **e**ngine **u**nnecessarily for **p**rofit."

A job applicant submits his **RESUME**, or "**R**ichly **e**xaggerated **s**aga of **u**tterly **m**eaningless **e**xperience."

At a store, a shopper discovers that **SERVICE** means "**S**ullen **e**mployees **r**arely **v**isible and **i**gnoring **c**ustomers **e**verywhere," while the manufacturer's **WARRANTY** is a "**W**orthless **a**ssurance **r**arely **r**elevant **a**nd **n**ever **t**o **y**ou."

Prior to his retirement as host of *The Tonight Show,* Johnny Carson offered an appreciative audience a bunch of creative acronyms, of which the following three may have been the funniest:

CABLE means "**C**hannels **a**bound, **b**ut **l**ittle **e**ntertainment."

IN-LAWS means "**I**f **n**earing, **l**eave **a**t **w**arp **s**peed."

PLAYMATES means "**P**retty **l**adies **a**nd **y**oung **m**en **a**morously **t**ouching **e**very **s**taple."

A competition in *New York* magazine asked for a capsule review forming an acronym of the work critiqued. Sixty-six entries were printed, including my own submission: " '**S**cary, **w**eird **e**xperience!' **e**nthuses *News*. '**E**pic **y**arn **t**hat's **o**peratic, **d**eadly **d**rama.' " But I must concede that the submission of Thomas M. Cope of Los Angeles is superior, deservedly winning first prize: " '**A**dolescents **n**eed **i**diotic **mo**vies, **a**nd **L**andis **h**as **o**bliged **us**'—**S**iskel, **E**bert."

Since Britain's *New Statesman & Society* began publication in 1913, every issue of the weekly newsmagazine has contained a wordplay competition. Sometimes the premise is acronymic.

One such contest invited readers to "imagine that Shakespeare's titles were acronyms." Among the suggestions: "**H**e **a**gonizes, **M**um **l**usts, **e**verybody **t**alks" (submitted by Naomi Marks), "**M**urky **a**trocities **c**ommitted **b**y **e**asily **t**empted **h**usband" (Peter Norman), and "**O**verblown **t**ragedy **h**as **e**thnic **l**over **l**osing **o**ut" (David Brain).

On another occasion, the magazine requested "acronyms for itinerant randies on the continent of Europe." The submissions proved to be so graphic, and in such dubious taste, that the editors announced that they had banned the results! This was the only competition, of about twenty-five hundred to that point, to meet that sad fate. Ultimately, however, some entries *were* printed, of which this one, submitted by Mack Donald, is representative: "**C**an

oral **p**leasuring **e**ver **n**ullify **h**and **a**nd **g**enital **e**xcitement? **N**o!"

Acronyms of the Future?

At the beginning of Chapter 4, we posed this question: How does an acronym enter popular usage, gain acceptance, and—sometimes—become a "real" word, part of our language?

We might gain some insight into the answer if we imagine two golfers conversing in the locker room of a suburban country club, where members must identify themselves to a guard in order to be admitted.

"Where's Fred?"

"His membership expired. But they found him trying to sneak in again. He was **c**aught **w**ithout **a** **c**ard."

"You mean they **CWAC**ed him?"

"That's right."

"It had to happen. Poor Fred. He was a sitting duck."

Well, this incident didn't really occur. But it *could* have. Thus can an acronym be created, and slip naturally into popular parlance.

We saw in Chapter 4 that **yuppie** gained wide currency, while scores of other sociological or lifestyle acronyms, some more clever and amusing, sank into obscurity. Why do some coinages survive, while others become mere nonce words?

The answer may lie in another question: Does the coinage meet a genuine *need* for a new word? Some years ago, an enthusiastic environmentalist dreamed up **rejase,** from "**re**use **j**unk **a**s **s**omething **e**lse." But we already have the perfectly serviceable word *recycle.* So "rejasing" was unceremoniously consigned to the linguistic landfill, where it presumably is biodegrading even as you read.

In 1984, a Britisher coined a word for self-pity: **ploms,** from "**p**oor **l**ittle **o**ld **m**e **s**yndrome." Clever, but once again a need for a new word was not met, and the expression failed to catch on.

Surely the authority on funny neologisms is comedian Rich Hall, who invented "sniglets"—words that don't appear in dictionaries, but should. He collected numerous specimens from H.B.O. viewers and compiled them into several paperback books.

The first of these volumes, *Sniglets* (1984), contained the suggested word **piyan,** from "**p**lus **i**f **y**ou **a**ct **n**ow." Its creator defined it as "any miscellaneous item thrown in on a late night television ad."

Here are some of my own suggestions for acronyms that have not yet entered the language but (perhaps) deserve to do so:

TOOTL, a verb; to be placed **t**otally **o**ut **o**f **t**he **l**oop. ("I didn't have any say in the matter. They tootled me.")

AW, BOSS!, short for **a w**hole **b**unch **o**f **s**tupid **s**tuff. All those distasteful tasks at work.

TRIPE, for **t**his **r**eally **i**s **p**retty **e**xciting, the opposite of the intended meaning. Use the expansion to say something nice about something you hate. Only those who know the code will understand.

TA-TA, meaning **t**hat's **a**ll **t**here **a**re. The perfect announcement when you complete a large pile of work and head for home.

At a film with a slow or nonexistent plot, you could vent your frustrations by shouting "**GOWI!**"—an acronym for "**G**et **o**n **w**ith **i**t!" (sounds a bit like an Indian war cry). You might have been warned by a review that said, "**N**ovel, **i**ngenious **p**remise, **bu**t **u**ltimately **d**isappointing," or **NIP-BUD**. A really good movie, on the other hand, **k**nocks **y**our **s**ocks **o**ff, or **KYSO**.

Here are a few marketing ideas:

A fundamentalist group might publish a shocking exposé called ***S**ex **a**nd **t**he **A**merican **N**ewlywed* (***SATAN***). A childrearing guide could be titled ***S**traight **T**alk **o**n **R**aising **K**ids* (***STORK***).

On television, a good name for a documentary featuring firsthand accounts of plantation adventures during the Civil War might be ***L**ife **a**s **W**e **S**ee **I**t,* or ***LAWSI***. An espionage drama could be titled ***W**e **H**ave **o**ur **S**pies **E**verywhere,* or ***WHOSE?***

Madison Avenue is always ready to capitalize on a trend. A hay fever remedy could be named **ACHOOO!**, for **A**llergy **C**ontrol—**H**alting **O**bnoxious **O**lfactory **O**rganisms. A sedative might be **SLAB**, for **S**leep **L**ike **a** **B**aby.

Finally, if you have a spouse or child who is chronically forgetful when leaving home, try my acronymic reminder: **TAMALE**, which stands for "**T**ake **a** **m**inute **a**nd **l**ook **e**verywhere."

Acronyms as Social Comment

The zenith of facetious acronyming is the extended essay. It's a new literary genre we call "**Mul**tiple **a**cronymia: **l**engthy, **i**nventive, **c**lever **e**xcursions," or **MALICE**.

In Chapter 3, we noted that mystics of the past saw acronyms lurking everywhere, and attempted to tease profound hidden meanings from every sentence and text. Maybe they were not so far off, after all. We contend that every important issue confronting our society—from love to money to politics—can be reduced to acronymic form and thereby solved.

The following brief commentary should help prove my point.

Same **O**ld **S**ong **a**nd **D**ance!
(**SO SAD!**)

True friends are dependable. They are **p**atient **a**nd **l**ong-**s**uffering (**PALS**). Those who consistently exceed expectations merit a place of honor among the **g**reat **a**nd **n**ear-**g**reat (**GANG**).

Tragically, however, they can sometimes let you down. When that happens, it helps to remember that **p**eople **a**re **r**ather **t**houghtless, **n**ot **e**vil **r**eally (**PARTNER**).

Some folks are **s**mug, **l**azy, **o**ver **t**he **h**ill (**SLOTH**). They hang around listlessly even when you tell them to **g**et **o**ut **a**nd **d**o **s**omething (**GOADS**). But don't be excessively loyal. After all, a few people will always be **f**ar **o**ut **o**f **l**ine (**FOOL**). Those who fail to shape up must be sternly cautioned: "**Y**ou're **o**n **y**our **o**wn (**YO-YO**)!"

Take teenagers, for instance. A youngster finds someone **b**lond **a**nd **b**lue-**e**yed (**BABE**). "**S**eems **l**ike **a** **n**ice **g**irl (**SLANG**)!," he concludes. They become convinced they are **o**ptimally **r**ight **f**or **e**ach **o**ther (**ORFEO**). But be warned: **L**ove **a**t **f**irst **s**ight (**LAFS**) isn't always what it's cracked up to be.

Today, young people naively assume they can **l**ive **o**n **l**ove **a**lone (**LOLA**). They'll tell each other: "Let's **g**o **o**n **o**ur **f**irst **i**nstincts (**GOOFI**)." But that's an expensive mistake. In **a** **m**oment **o**f **r**ash **e**agerness (**AMORE**), they can hurt themselves for years to follow and invite **a** **l**ot **o**f **h**eavy **a**buse (**ALOHA**). That truth will dawn only when they are hit by the **c**old **l**ight **o**f **d**ay (**CLOD**). At that point, they are likely to exclaim, "**T**hanks; **I** **n**eeded **t**hat (**TINT**)!"

The first thing they should tell themselves is: "**G**et **o**ur **s**upport **s**ystems **i**n **p**lace (**GOSSIP**)!" But they usually just don't think about the high costs of survival these days.

So many things are **p**riced **o**ut **o**f **r**each (**POOR**), especially when you've got **a** **m**ob **o**f **k**ids (**AMOK**). You wind up trying to **l**ive **o**n **a**lmost **n**othing

(**LOAN**). Just getting by can require an **e**xcruciating **e**ffort **o**f **w**ill (**EE-OW!**). These harsh realities become clear when you write those monthly checks and see the dreaded words "**P**ay **t**o **t**he **o**rder **o**f . . . (**PTTOO!**)."

In the free-spending 1980s, everyone wanted to **t**ry **a**nything **o**nce (**TAO**). Even then, we knew that **s**ome **p**eople **a**re **n**ever **s**atisfied (**SPANS**). **S**ex **a**nd **d**rug **e**scapades (**SADE**) were everywhere. Don't those annual Aspen skiing vacations now **s**eem **l**ike **a** **l**ot **o**f **m**oney (**SLALOM**)?

Yes, sometimes you've got to **s**truggle **t**o **e**arn **a** **l**iving (**STEAL**). At times you may even be tempted to bid farewell to **t**hings **a**s **t**hey **a**re (**TA-TA**).

Cheer up! When you're depressed, remember to **l**ook **o**n **t**he **b**right **s**ide (**LOT BS**). But if you entertain fantasies of easy wealth, don't forget: "He who hungers for **p**ie **i**n **t**he **s**ky/Should ponder the acronym crafted thereby."

Why are Americans hurting? It's because of the fallacies and myths our leaders believe and practice. The prevalence of such misguided economic and social notions is a **s**ad **c**ommentary **o**n **o**ur **t**ime (**SCOOT**).

These guys think they can **w**alk **o**n **w**ater (**WOW**). With exaggerated confidence they tell each other, "**Y**ou **a**re **s**o **i**ndubitably **r**ight (**YASIR**)" and "**T**hat's **w**hat **I** **t**hink (**TWIT**)." Yet they attempt to **w**alk **a** **f**ine **l**ine (**WAFL**), straddling the fence on every issue.

But they are **h**opelessly **o**utside **r**eality, **r**hyme, **o**r reason (**HORROR**). Hearing what politicians say on the news, you probably exclaim: "**T**his **r**eally **is** **b**izarre (**TRIB**)!" and "**T**hat **is** **s**imply **n**ot **t**rue (**TISN'T**)!"

I keep **h**oping **a**gainst **h**ope (**HAH**) that politicians will learn **t**here **is** **a** **r**ight **a**nswer (**TIARA**), and even the difference between **w**rong **a**nd **r**ight (**WAR**). Maybe one of these days they'll **g**et **u**p **t**o **s**peed (**GUTS**), summon the courage to identify the real issue, and **hi**t **i**t **h**ead **o**n (**HI HO**).

That **r**eally **is** **a** **l**augh (**TRIAL**). The problems we face today are a **d**ifferent **o**rder **o**f **m**agnitude (**DOOM**). Their litany has become so familiar that I'm **b**ored **o**ut **o**f **m**y **s**kull (**BOOMS**). Sometimes I suspect that we are **b**etter **o**ff **n**ot **k**nowing (**BONK**).

CHAPTER 9

❖

Remarkably Entertaining Games And Recreational Diversions (REGARD)

Throughout this book, and especially in the previous chapter, you have encountered samples of acronymic creativity and humor.

"The alphabet provides a natural basis for many types of games and word play," notes Tony Augarde in *The Oxford Guide to Word Games.*

So we herewith present a collection of **m**iscellaneous **a**cronymic **s**tuff **t**o **o**bfuscate, **d**elight, **o**r **n**onplus (**MASTODON,** for short). This chapter is a treasury of fun and games, literary diversions, intriguing trivia, and assorted ephemera.

The Acronym Game

This is an entertaining party game or a solitary diversion. You don't even need to buy anything. Here are the rules:

The moderator cites a word or a phrase, and the

players must create a self-defining, or otherwise appropriate, sentence from its initial letters. For example, the word **map** could be "defined" as "**m**arks **a**ctual **p**laces."

The **A**cronym **G**ame (**TAG**, for short) is an educational activity for children and a mental challenge for adults. It helps build vocabulary skills. For crossword and Scrabble enthusiasts, it's a stimulating change of pace. In a group, competition can be among individuals or teams. Players may either immediately call out their answers or practice solutions on paper first.

Nouns seem to work best as clues. Long words, not surprisingly, are harder than short ones. Certain letters, such as K, Q, X, Y, and Z, are tougher than others. One potentially interesting variant is to use as clues the first names or surnames of people who are present—or absent!

Briefing for judges:

There **a**ren't **r**eally **a**ny **r**ight **a**nswers (**TARARA!**). The audience may vote for the best coinage or choose to appoint a judge. Criteria are aptness, wit, humor, and tendentious social comment. General silliness and laughter also indicate a likely winner.

For other principles that govern whether a coinage is legitimate or illegitimate, and for hints on evaluating its quality, see our acronym rules in Chapter 2.

So let's play TAG! Here are some examples to get you started. Suggested solutions are in Appendix I.

For more words, grab any nearby periodical or book. Good luck. May the best acronyms win!

Basic level—short words:

HAT
WAR
NOSE
SHOP

Advanced level—longer words, phrases, names, titles:

KNIFE
LAWYER
MIDNIGHT
SHAMPOO
CYRANO
TIMEPIECE

Palindromic Acronyms

Palindromes are words or phrases that spell the same backward and forward. They are perennial favorites of word lovers.

The most familiar palindromic acronym is undoubtedly *radar*. It's appropriate because the word, like the signal, goes both ways! Short palindromic acronyms, such as **DAD** and **WOW,** are abundant, and have numerous variant expansions. The challenge is to find (or create) longer examples.

Dmitri Borgmann's *Language on Vacation* cites **RAFAR** (**r**adio **a**utomated **f**acsimile **a**nd **r**eproduction) and **MOCOM** (**Mo**bile **Com**mand, a syllabic Army acronym). **MADDAM** is **M**acromodule **a**nd **D**igital **D**ifferential **A**nalyzer **M**achine, as well as **M**ultiplexed **A**nalog to **D**igital, **D**igital to **A**nalog **M**ultiplexed. (Both terms are from data processing.)

Can you find, or devise, a longer palindromic acronym?

Other Alphabet Games

In Chapter 1, we briefly noted what we dubbed "phonemic abbreviation." This is the process that turns letters into punned renderings of the words or syllables of a phrase or sentence. The game can be fun for children—and for adults who enjoy silly wordplay. Here are some examples:

FUNEX is "Have you any eggs?"

OUQT is "Oh, you cutie."

Often cited is the verse: "**YYUR YYUB ICUR YY4 ME.**" The translation is easy if you say "two Y's."

Working from this principle, cartoonist William Steig wrote and illustrated two books for children: *CDB!* (*See the Bee!*, 1968) and *CDC?* (*See the Sea?*, 1984). In one of Steig's drawings, a woman asks her scratching spouse, "**U F N H?**" He replies, "**I F N L-R-G.**"

In *The Game of Words,* Willard Espy provides a glossary for what he calls "A.B.C. Language." It provides a vocabulary, he notes, "about the size of a bushman's, though less practical." Many of Espy's other "recreational linguistics" books provide compositions in A.B.C., often in verse.

A similar diversion is suggested by the Postal Service's official two-letter state abbreviations. Consider a session involving a patient and his Freudian psychotherapist. (Note: Ethical considerations allow us to report only one side of the dialogue.)

"HI, MD. MI MA OR PA AR IL. ID IN ME OK? KS MS? WY? OH!"

One promising venue for collecting specimens of this sort of wordplay is the vanity license plate, where restrictions on the number of characters—a maximum of between six and eight—force drivers to be creative in order to spell out a message. Some genuine (but only partially punned) examples: **SUZ E Q, B-Z BEE, LUV U 2, IN XTC.**

Acrostic Verse and Song

In Chapter 3, we discussed the early history of the acrostic—a literary composition, usually in verse, in which a word or phrase or sentence is created by the first letter of each line. The ancestor of the modern acronym, alphabetic and word/sentence acrostics date back to the seventh century B.C.E.

Literati scorn the form as contrived, and it is now generally regarded as archaic, or at least old-fashioned. But for millennia, acrostic poems served as tributes and as romantic missives. A few major poets even dabbled in the form.

The following example, a civic-minded encomium by a Mr. Leroy R. Blackwell, appeared in 1856 in a slim volume published by the author himself, which included similarly effusive accolades to James Buchanan and Millard Fillmore. Its treacly sentiments may give you an idea of why the form is now out of style.

Proud and towering to the skies,
Here houses after houses rise,
Infolding in their each embrace
Lovely girls adorned with grace.
Accompanied are thy sons and daughters,
Delightful too thy streets and waters;
Extending thy influence wide,
Learned men in thee reside.
Protect thy people one and all,
Hear them when for aid they call,
In thee let them live and die,
And from thee soar above the sky.

A few popular songs are constructed in acrostic form, such as the sentimental musical tribute to "**M-O-T-H-E-R**" ("**M** is for the million things she gave me. . . ."), written by Howard Johnson and Theodore Morse in 1915, and "**L-O-V-E**" ("L is for the way you look at me. . . ."), written by Milt Gabler and Bert Kaempfert in 1964, and popularized by Nat King Cole.

Verses can also employ the *last* letter of each line, a form called a *telestich,* or even a set of *middle* letters, which creates a *mesostich.* Combinations produce a *double* or *triple acrostic.* But a discussion of these variations would lead us astray from our main subject.

An acrostic can be as brief as a single word, where each letter stands for another word, as in **FIDO,** a numismatists' mnemonic for **f**reaks, **i**rregularities, **d**efects, **o**ddities. Here the border between the acrostic and the acronym begins to blur.

Crossword puzzles, word squares, and Double-Crostic puzzles are among the games that employ the acrostic principle. For more alphabetical diversions, see the books listed at the end of the bibiliography in Appendix II.

CHAPTER 10

The Ultimate Best Acronyms (TUBA)

We are approaching a conclusion. We will now consider the record for the lengthiest acronym, present the award winners, and peek into our crystal ball to envision the future of acronymy.

The Acronym Acronym

Not surprisingly, more than one wit has attempted to devise an expansion for the word **acronym.**

The New York Times once editorialized, presumably tongue-in-cheek, in favor of organizing an **A**ction **C**ommittee to **R**eform **O**ur **N**ation's **Y**outh **M**orals. A genuine group named itself **A**llied **C**itizens **R**epresenting **O**ther **N**ew **Y**ork **M**inorities.

More elegant are attempts to make the word *self-defining.* Consider the following candidates:

"**A**lphabet **c**haracters **r**epresenting **o**ther **n**ames **y**ielding **m**eaning" was the consensus of the students of Jo-Ann M. Burns, a Newport, R.I., high school English teacher who uses acronyms as an instructional tool.

Another nominee is "**A**cceptable **c**ontractions of **r**andomly **o**rganized **n**ames **y**ielding **m**eritorious **s**pontaneity."

"**A c**oinage **r**einforcing **o**r **n**ourishing **y**our **m**emory." The creation of B. G. Dilworth, a New York literary agent.

And perhaps the most appealing: "**A c**ontrived **r**eduction **o**f **n**omenclature **y**ielding **m**nemonics." In 1959, this felicitous coinage was attributed to John Mills Martin and Christopher Vickery.

The Longest Acronym?

At twenty-six letters, the U.S. Navy's **COMSUBCOMNELMCOMHEDSUPPACT**, for **Com**mander, **Sub**ordinate **Com**mand, **N**aval Forces, **E**astern Atlantic and **M**editerranean, **Com**mander **Head**quarters **Supp**ort **Act**ivities, is "said to be the longest English-language acronym," according to the *Acronyms, Initialisms & Abbreviations Dictionary.*

Another sesquipedalian specimen is **PUMCODOXPURSACOMLOPAR** (twenty-one letters), for **Pu**lse-**M**odulated **Co**herent **Do**ppler-Effect

X-Band **Pu**lse-**R**epetition **S**ynthetic-**A**rray Pulse **Com**pression Side **Lo**be **P**lanar **A**rray.

The Russian syllabic acronym **NIIOMTPLABOPARMBETZHELBETRABSBOMONIMONIMONKONOTDTEKHSTROMONT** is sixty letters in Roman characters and fifty-four in the original Cyrillic. We won't burden you with the full Russian expansion, but its English translation (per the *Concise Dictionary of Soviet Terminology*) is "The laboratory for shuttering, reinforcement, concrete and ferro-concrete operations, for composite-monolithic and monolithic constructions, of the Department of the Technology of Building-assembly operations of the Scientific Research Institute of the Organization for Building Mechanization and Technical Aid of the Academy of Building and Architecture of the U.S.S.R."

In 1968, this abbreviation appeared in the Soviet humor magazine *Krokodil.* It apparently journeyed West until it reached the editors of *The Guinness Book of World Records,* who promptly pronounced it the world's longest acronym.

TUBA (The Ultimate Best Acronym) Awards

Which acronyms are *best*? In our grading system (Chapter 2), we bestow highest honors on those coinages that form a genuine word that is natural, logical, and appropriate to its source. These elegant creations are *quality acronyms.*

The problem with the above examples is that they are *meaningless.* They may well be pronounceable and lengthy, but so what? Obviously, a coiner can produce a potentially infinite number of letter or syllable combinations simply by stringing words together.

On the other hand, it's easy to find lots of short (three- and four-letter) combinations that are meaningful. So although length is a criterion, the extended acronym must also make sense.

The following candidates receive Honorable Mentions:

The now apparently defunct **C**ommittee **o**n **N**ational **S**tudent **C**itizenship **i**n **E**very **N**ational **C**ase of **E**mergency, or **CONSCIENCE**, at ten letters, is cited by A. Ross Eckler, the editor of *Word Ways,* as an unusually long and meaningful acronym.

In 1964, a K.G.B. "disinformation" campaign attempted to discredit F.B.I. director Hoover by fabricating correspondence implying that he was involved in a homosexual relationship. The chief assigned the agency to snoop into the attempted smear. The investigation bore the code name **REPULSE**, which supposedly stood for "**R**ussian **e**fforts to **p**ublish **u**nsavory **l**ove **s**ecrets of **E**dgar." An F.B.I. spokesperson confirmed to me that REPULSE existed, but denied (well, what would you expect?) that the name, at the time it was chosen, was an acronym. The ingenious redefinition apparently came later.

Perhaps the most frequently cited example of an

apt acronym concerns high-profile former auto executive Lee Iacocca, whose surname can be interpreted to announce "**I a**m **C**hairman **o**f **C**hrysler **C**orporation of **A**merica."

Chance—or design? You be the judge. In response to my inquiry, a Chrysler spokesperson responded: "So far, no one has taken credit for creating this acronym, and we attribute the phrase to pure coincidence." (It works nicely as a spelling mnemonic, too.)

At the end of 1992, Mr. Iacocca retired. What now? Well, perhaps his name can be redefined to mean "**I a**in't **C**hairman **o**f **C**hrysler **C**orporation **a**nymore!"

A special "Best *Non*-Acronym Award" goes to **ABCDEFGHIJ**, a World War II organization. It stood for **A**utomobile **B**uilders' **C**ombination **D**esigned **E**specially **f**or **G**etting **H**itler, **I**ncluding **J**apan.

Now, here are the winners of The First Annual TUBA Awards. (Flourish of trumpets—or tubas!) The listing is alphabetical. None was mentioned earlier. Winners of this soon-to-be-coveted honor will be inducted into the Acronymic Hall of Fame and may (or may not) receive a trophy in the shape of a tuba.

ALOHA, **A**boriginal **L**ands **o**f **H**awaiian **A**ncestry. A campaign to compensate native inhabitants for property confiscated from their predecessors by colonists and rulers of the islands prior to 1893.

BEHEMOTH, **B**ig **E**lectronic **H**uman-**E**nergized **M**achine . . . **O**nly **T**oo **H**eavy. In 1992, Ohio writer Steven Roberts equipped a bicycle with several computers and so many other gizmos that the vehicle wound up costing $1.2 million and weighing 580 pounds.

BOADICEA, **B**ritish **O**verseas **A**irways **D**igital **I**nformation **C**omputer for **E**lectronic **A**utomation. Boadicea was the British "warrior queen" who led an unsuccessful revolt against invading Romans in the year 61. (BOAC is now British Airways.)

BO PEEP, **B**angor **O**range **P**osition **E**stimating **E**quipment for **P**astures. An electronic beeper used by shepherds to track their flocks. Bangor is a city in Wales.

BORN FREE, **B**uild **O**ptions, **R**enew **N**orms, **F**ree **R**oles through **E**ducational **E**quity, a student career project.

CLASSMATE, **C**omputer **L**anguage to **A**id and **S**imulate **S**cientific, **M**athematical, **a**nd **T**echnical **E**ducation.

COSA NOSTRA, **C**omputer-**O**riented **S**ystem **a**nd **N**ewly **O**rganized **S**torage-**t**o-**R**etrieval **A**pparatus. (Special Mention for quirkiness.)

EGRESS, **E**mergency **G**lobal **R**escue, **E**scape, and **S**urvival **S**ystem. (NASA.)

GOLDBERG, **G**enerally **O**perational **L**inear **D**igit-controlled **B**iphase **E**lectrical **R**etardance **G**ate. (IBM.)

HOLMES, **H**ome **O**ffice **L**arge **M**ajor **E**nquiry **S**ystem, a British crime-tracking computer system.

HOT-SHOT, **H**ydrogen-**O**xygen **T**urbine: **S**uper-**H**igh **O**perating **T**emperatures.

LOBSTER, **L**ong-term **O**cean **B**ottom **S**ettlement **T**est for **E**ngineering **R**esearch. (A Navy project.)

PARENTS, **P**eople of **A**merica **R**esponding to **E**ducational **N**eeds of **T**oday's **S**ociety. (Now defunct, unfortunately.)

PASSAGES, **P**laces for **A**dult **S**urvivors of **S**exual **A**ssault to **G**row and **E**volve **S**afely.

RESCUE, **R**ecovery **E**mploying **S**torage **C**hute **U**sed in **E**mergencies. (An inflatable aircraft wing.)

SANTA, **S**ouvenir **a**nd **N**ovelty **T**rade **A**ssociation.

SURFSIDE, **S**mall **U**nified **R**eactor **F**acility with **S**ystems for **I**sotopes, **D**esalting, and **E**lectricity. (A New York State nuclear-powered plant designed to turn ocean water into fresh water.)

SWIFT-ANSWER, **S**pecial **W**ord **I**ndexed **F**ull **T**ext **A**lpha **N**umeric **S**torage **w**ith **E**asy **R**etrieval. (Computer software.)

Acronymic Megatrends and Future Shock

Will the art of acronymy survive?

What if acronyms, initialisms, and other abbreviations proliferate to the extent that they duplicate and encroach upon one another? Will they self-destruct from sheer overuse? Will the critics we heard from in Chapter 1 succeed in their campaign to wipe them out?

Fortunately, we have another view.

"Acronyms thrive in the hothouse environment of literacy," contends lexicographer John Algeo. "In the past, their greatest use has been among communities with a high regard for the value of the written word."

This observation is surely true. In Chapter 3, we observed that acronyms and abbreviations appealed to Greek and Roman writers, to Jewish scholars, and to other literate people throughout history. We noted the literary use of acrostics. And we discovered that acronyms were inherent in the very birth of alphabetic writing.

That's a position quite different from that of the people who denounce acronyms as an assault on language. To the contrary, we maintain that acronyms are characteristic of advanced civilizations and highly intelligent minds. Those possessed, for example, by the readers of this book. Here indeed are the men and women of letters.

Professor Algeo waxes eloquent on the virtues of the art:

"In the making of acronyms there is a spirit of poetic playfulness. As perhaps the most easily made kind of word, the acronym gives scope for the impulse to creativity [and] lets Everyman indulge the impulse to be at once linguist and poet, to produce new words playfully."

He's right. Even as you read these words, someone is creating a new acronym. If you discover or invent a specimen not already captured in these pages, please write to me. Corrections or elaborations are also welcome. Perhaps I will use your contribution in a future edition of or sequel to *ACRONYMANIA*.

Don Hauptman
c/o Dell Publishing
1540 Broadway, 19th fl.
New York, NY 10036

In Greek, *logos* ("LOWG-us") is a potent and seminal word that has, among other meanings: thought, reason, definition, explanation, argument, principle, and *word.* ("In the beginning was the Word.") I hope you have found in this book all of those things, but especially **l**ots **o**f **g**ood **o**riginal **s**tuff—or **LOGOS**, for short!

APPENDIX I

Suggested Solutions for The Acronym Game

(See page 243)

I test-drove the game among language lovers attending "The Wonderful World of Words," an annual event at Mohonk Mountain House, New Paltz, N.Y. My thanks to all the clever people who participated, and who joined me in suggesting the following "answers" (in which all the letters of each "acronym" form words, and no extraneous words are added). Of course, these represent possibilities only. Your solutions may be even better.

Basic level—short words:

HAT

Head **a**ppropriately **t**opped
Headgear **a**bove **t**resses
Human **a**natomy **t**opper
Homburg **a**cross **t**oupee

WAR

Waging **a**rmed **r**ebellion
We **a**ggress **r**andomly
Weapons **a**nd **r**uin

NOSE

Natural **o**lfactory **s**ensing **e**quipment
Nasal **o**rifice **s**mells **e**verything

SHOP

Spend **h**eavily **o**n **p**resents
Save **h**eaps **o**n **p**urchases
Sales **h**ave **o**ften **p**rofited

Advanced level—longer words, phrases, names, titles:

KNIFE

Keen, **n**ecessary **i**mplement **f**or **e**ating
Kitchen **n**uisance **i**n **f**elon's **e**mploy

LAWYER

Legal **a**dviser **w**ho's **y**our **e**xpensive **r**epresentative
Legal **a**ssociate **w**as **y**oung **e**ager **r**ecruit

MIDNIGHT

Mysterious **i**nterlude **d**uring **n**ight **i**s **g**houlish: **H**alloween **t**ricks?
Man, **i**t's **d**ark—**n**ow **I**'m **g**etting **h**ellishly **t**ired!

SHAMPOO

Soft **h**air **a**llows **m**e **p**ossibility **o**f **o**versoaping
Styling **h**air **a**nd **m**aking **p**erm **o**verly **o**pulent

CYRANO

Clever **y**uppie **r**oué's **a**nonymous **n**ovel **o**ratory
Call **y**our **r**hinologist: **a** **n**ew **o**ddity

Choose **y**our **r**apier—**a**nd **n**o **o**ther
Chum, **y**our **r**ipostes **a**re **n**ever **o**btuse!

TIMEPIECE

This **i**ndicates **m**inutes; **e**very **p**art **i**s **e**xpertly crafted—**e**gads!
There **i**s **m**y **e**ternal **p**roblem: **I** **e**xpect **c**hronological **e**vents
Ticking **i**nstrument **m**arking **e**ternity's **p**assage **i**ncrementally, **e**ventually **c**ollapsing **e**ntropically

APPENDIX II

Sources and References

Among my sources for the citations in *ACRONYMANIA* were newspaper and magazine articles, the references listed below (among others), people working in specialized professions and industries, and the collections of fellow acronym enthusiasts (as noted in the Acknowledgments).

For the "real" words and mythical acronyms discussed in Chapter 4, my sources included *The Oxford English Dictionary, The Random House Dictionary of the English Language,* and numerous etymological dictionaries and books of word origins. For colloquial usage, several standard dictionaries of slang and euphemism proved helpful. For historical material, I consulted *Benét's Reader's Encyclopedia, Brewer's Dictionary of Phrase and Fable,* and many other sources.

If you need further information, following are some of the abbreviation references I consulted. This is a selected listing, which I attempted to restrict to books in print. But out-of-print volumes, if needed, may often be found in reference libraries and secondhand bookstores. One caveat: A publishing industry cliché is that a directory is out of date the day it comes off the press.

Note that terminology is often used loosely or

incorrectly. Despite the phrase *Dictionary of Acronyms* as part of a title, the volume may well include initialisms and other types of abbreviation, along with coinages pronounceable as words. Acronyms and initialisms are invariably cobbled together, with initialisms tending to constitute the bulk of the listings.

In addition to general reference works, virtually every field, profession, and discipline has its own specialized reference volumes, either specifically of abbreviations or of *all* kinds of terminology. The latter type sometimes contains a separate abbreviation glossary. Titles of such books often include the words *Dictionary, Glossary, Encyclopedia, Word Book, Terms,* or *Terminology.*

A note of caution: Although these volumes supply expansions, they only occasionally provide definitions or explanations, or any sort of detail or context. Thus you may learn that **CISAM** means "**c**ompressed **i**ndex **s**equential **a**ccess **m**ethod," but *not* what that phrase means or even the field in which it is used!

In Chapter 3, we noted that the first book of this type was published in 1494. The trend accelerated in the United Kingdom and the United States during the nineteenth century, and really got rolling after World War II. Most of those volumes are, of course, no longer in print. Their listings are out of date, and they are of interest only for historical reasons.

APPENDIX II

General Abbreviation Dictionaries

The major resource is the massive, multivolume *Acronyms, Initialisms & Abbreviations Dictionary (A.I.A.D.),* published annually by Gale Research. Intended primarily for reference libraries, it consists of three volumes listing more than 520,000 terms in 3,844 pages—all weighing in at a backache-inducing nineteen pounds! At this writing, it is priced at $235. Gale also churns out a number of supplements and spinoffs that catalog abbreviations in various ways.

A more manageable and affordable reference is Ralph deSola's *Abbreviations Dictionary* (CRC Press, 160,000 entries), which has been through many editions and contains a series of helpful appendices for business, school, and home use.

Other volumes that are reasonably priced and in print are the *Concise Dictionary of Acronyms and Initialisms* by Stuart W. Miller (Facts On File, 5,000 entries); *The Penguin Dictionary of Abbreviations* by John Paxton (paperback, 40,000 entries, originally published in the United Kingdom as *Everyman's Dictionary of Abbreviations*); *The New American Dictionary of Abbreviations* by Mary deVries (Signet paperback, 10,000 entries); and the small and inexpensive *Webster's Guide to Abbreviations* (Merriam-Webster, 12,000 entries).

At this writing, the two most recent general reference books are as follows: *The Oxford Dictionary of Abbreviations* (Oxford University Press, 19,000 entries), which includes both American and British usage; and *NTC's Dictionary of Acronyms and Abbreviations* (National Textbook Company, 2,100 entries), which supplies unusually detailed definitions, along with sample uses in context.

Perhaps the most unusual volume I encountered is *Abbreviations, Acronyms, Ciphers & Signs* (Gale Research), which consists entirely of reproductions of Library of Congress catalog cards for books, in every language, that deal in some way with these subjects. Only for the scholar or the insatiably curious.

Specialized Abbreviation Dictionaries

Wynwood Press publishes three specialized and reasonably priced paperbacks, the entries adapted from the *A.I.A.D.* (see above) database: *Dictionary of Business Acronyms, Dictionary of Computer and Telecommunications Acronyms,* and *Dictionary of Medical and Health Acronyms.* Each volume contains 20,000 to 30,000 entries.

McGraw-Hill publishes a similar set of references, both in paperback and hardcover, each compiled by Jerry M. Rosenberg, with the titles *McGraw-Hill Dictionary of Business Acronyms, Initials and Abbreviations; McGraw-Hill Dictionary of Information Technology & Computer Acronyms, Initials and Abbreviations;* and *McGraw-Hill Dictionary of Wall Street Acronyms, Initials and Abbreviations.* Each volume contains 10,000 to 15,000 entries.

Among the areas in which you will find abbreviation dictionaries: computers, medicine, the sciences, engineering, government, education, international organizations, communications, business and finance, library science, language and linguistics, and many others.

Guides to military and aerospace terminology have been published by the Defense Department, by each branch of the armed services, and by defense contractors such as McDonnell Douglas and Emhart. (In an effort to appear up-to-date, a 1964 volume was titled *Space-Age Acronyms*. Ironically, the phrase already sounds archaic.)

Finally, almost every language has its own dictionaries of abbreviations.

Resources

For hard-to-find reference books, try one of the following retailers:

The Dictionary Store carries specialized reference volumes in every field, including foreign languages. It publishes *The Dictionary Catalogue,* ($5.00) which is just what you'd expect from the title; 115 Fifth Avenue, New York, N.Y. 10003; 212-673-7400.

The Reference Book Center stocks both new and used titles; catalog available ($2.00); 175 Fifth Avenue, New York, N.Y. 10010; 212-677-2160.

Articles

Among the hundreds of articles I consulted, these were perhaps the most useful and interesting on acronymy in general:

"The Acronym and Its Congeners" by John Algeo. In *The First Lacus (Linguistic Association of Canada and the United States) Forum 1974* (published by Hornbeam Press, Columbia, S.C.).

"From 'AWOL' to 'VEEP': The Growth and Specialization of the Acronym," by S. V. Baum. *American Speech* (May 1955).

"Abbreviations and Acronyms in English Word-Formation" by Garland Cannon. *American Speech* (Summer 1989).

"Rewriting Initialisms: Folk Derviations and Linguistic Riddles" by Nicholas Howe. *The Journal of American Folklore* (April–June 1989).

"The Cult of Abbreviation" by Tom McArthur. *English Today* (July 1988). The chart accompanying this article anticipated and influenced my own taxonomy in Chapter 2.

"Initialism & Acronymania" by Ralph Slovenko. *The Journal of Psychiatry and Law* (Fall-Winter 1986).

Books on Language

Surprisingly, many books on language and linguistics, both scholarly and popular, touch upon acronyms only briefly, if at all.

One recent exception is *The Oxford Companion to the English Language* edited by Tom McArthur (Oxford University Press), wherein McArthur's article "The Cult of Abbreviation" appears, updated and in somewhat different form.

For alphabet play, the many books of Richard Lederer and Willard Espy contain acronyms, acrostics, and other letter games, as does *The Oxford Guide to Word Games* by Tony Augarde (Oxford University Press).

Two fine periodicals that specialize in recreational linguistics and that at times include acronyms and other alphabet games are *Word Ways* (Morristown, N.J.) and *Verbatim* (Old Lyme, Conn.).